Persian Service

The BBC and British Interests in Iran

Annabelle Sreberny and
Massoumeh Torfeh

I.B. TAURIS

LONDON · NEW YORK

Published in 2014 by I.B.Tauris & Co. Ltd
6 Salem Road, London W2 4BU
175 Fifth Avenue, New York NY 10010
www.ibtauris.com

Distributed in the United States and Canada Exclusively by
Palgrave Macmillan, 175 Fifth Avenue, New York NY 10010

International Library of Iranian Studies: 40

ISBN: 978 1 84885 981 4

A full CIP record for this book is available from the British Library
A full CIP record is available from the Library of Congress

Library of Congress Catalog Card Number: available

Typeset by 4word Ltd, Bristol

Printed and bound by CPI Group (UK) Ltd, Croydon CR0 4YY

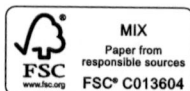

Contents

Introduction

The BBC World Service and Iran: 70 Years of the Delicate Dance

The mediascape of the twenty-first century is undergoing a major realignment. There are profound challenges to the long-taken-for-granted hegemony of Western media, particularly in the Middle East. A seriously engaged and globally focused Media Studies needs to re-engage with questions about the state, about propaganda and about new forms of diplomacy that may induce conflict. International relations have always included some elements of persuasion for home populations and propaganda for foreign nationals. At critical junctures, the rhetoric often outweighs the real relations and the drums of war are beaten across a plenitude of media platforms.

At the start of 2013, political relations between the Islamic Republic of Iran and Western democracies, Britain especially, were at their worst in years. The EU had followed the US in voting for increased sanctions as the only antidote to Iran's nuclear programme; there was little direct diplomacy; and inside Iran, more and more journalists and bloggers were arrested, making Iran one of the world's largest jailers of journalists and giving it a ranking of 174 of 179 countries in the World Press Freedom Index

2013.[1] And behind the 'real' relations, the mediated confusion – that is to say the media's confusion about Iran and the mediated confusion let loose on Western publics in particular about Iran – was getting worse.

International media channels, domestic broadcasters, websites and blogs all thrummed with negative anticipation about the worsening relations with Iran. And the responses of the Islamic Republic – across their own international and national broadcasting channels, their international travels and staged political theatre – were equally as much about corralling hearts and minds. International relations have turned into public diplomacy and international communication has made sign-masters of us all – the wars of words and images were already rolling. Within this tense and complex international scenario, relations between Britain and Iran were at rock-bottom. Formal diplomatic ties were severed in autumn 2011. Press TV, Iran's English-language television channel, had been ordered off the British Sky television platform, and the BBC Persian website remained blocked. Realpolitik and 'soft power'[2] had become intimately connected.

The BBC World Service practice of distance from government has emerged over time and not without a continuous struggle to claim and preserve control over the content of its broadcasts. Here we examine a particularly rich vein of World Service history, the establishment and development of the Persian-language service. The ethos of 'public service', a foundational value of the BBC, was thus discursively linked to its provision for the world and for Iran. This was developed in the epoch of the Empire Service, a time of overt utilization of external radio services as tools of propaganda, and has played a major role in relations between the UK and the Persian-speaking world at crucial political conjunctures. Iranians have listened to the BBC with scepticism, but also regarded the Persian Service as one of their most trusted sources of news and information. The recent 2007 Foreign and Commonwealth Office (FCO)[3] allocation of funds to the development of Arabic television and Persian television reveals how central the Middle East region

– and Iran in particular – remains to British political and economic interests. The proposed changes to World Service funding, with responsibility shifting from the FCO to the BBC itself from 2014, is a most significant structural change and we have to wait to see what impact, if any, it has on the Persian Service.

Framed by the changing nature of public diplomacy, this book explores one strand of connection within British–Iranian relations, the 70-year story of the Persian-language provision of the BBC and the Iranian responses. This book focuses specifically on the Persian services of the BBC World Service, which consisted initially only of radio but later included the internet and then television. We explore how the Persian services have dealt with and weathered attempts at political pressure from the British government, as well as rebutting pressure from various Iranian regimes to alter its coverage. We explore how the BBC World Service has progressively moved from a position that could be described as a channel of propaganda to playing a role in public diplomacy, later engaging in the new 'cultural diplomacy', terms which we unpack in Chapter 1.

We analyse how the BBC Persian Service itself became involved in five critical moments in British–Iranian relations: the removal of Reza Shah Pahlavi in 1941; the UK–Iran oil negotiations during 1948–53; the Iranian Revolution of 1979; broadcasting to Afghanistan 1980–2012; and, finally, the establishment of BBC Persian TV (BBC PTV) and confrontation with the Islamic Republic 2009–12. These periods of crisis have been chosen intentionally to explore the relationship between the British government and BBC Persian Service, and whether and how the former exerted pressure on the latter to communicate messages to Iranians that suited British foreign policy rather than broadcasting best practice. We also explore the responses by the Iranian political system, monarchical and theocratic, to the BBC and how the organization reacted. Thus this volume is not a complete history of the BBC Persian services, but an analysis of key moments in the shifting dynamics of power between the broadcaster and the government of the day.

This book hopes to contribute to a better understanding of the changing nature of British diplomacy and the broader implications of the nexus between government and international broadcasting, specifically between the FCO and the BBC. The work also sheds light on the twists and turns in British–Iranian relations in the five chosen periods of crisis and the way the BBC Persian Service was caught up in bilateral politics, whether it wanted to be or not.

But analysis of these complex relations does not mean our endorsement or approval of all of BBC Persian content. Indeed, this book does not include systematic analysis of BBC Persian Service's coverage of issues, including coverage of Iran. That would be fascinating but we leave it to others to develop this. However, we would make the point that *all* media systems manifest some of the socio-cultural attitudes of their country, so that simplistic analysis which charges the BBC with upholding British values is hardly novel.

The book also reveals how Iranians – as government officials and as a broader audience – perceived and perceive the relationship between the BBC and the British government. It reveals many attempts by Iranian politicians themselves to influence the BBC, it explores the ongoing inability of Iranian officials to believe that such a significant broadcaster can be independent of government control, and it shows how the BBC Persian Service from its start has been implicated in political relations between Iran and Britain.

Until recently, comparatively little research had been conducted on the World Service as a whole,[4] even less on the BBC Persian Service. Much of the research for this book was undertaken as part of the 'Tuning In' project on the BBC World Service, supported by the Arts and Humanities Research Council (AHRC).[5] Two primary sources of material have been used. In the first place the work depends centrally on the archives of the FCO at the National Archives in Kew Gardens, which include military and intelligence reports, and the BBC Written Archives at Caversham. Massoumeh Torfeh undertook most of the historical research and analysis, spending inordinate amounts of time in both places and becoming excited at the start of each year in expectation of the new Foreign Office (FO) documents that would be released. Over the years of the project, these included several documents that had never before been published relating to British views of Reza Shah, to the Anglo–American planning of the coup in 1953 and to the discussions relating to the revolution of 1979.[6] Throughout the volume, all FO documents noted are from the National Archives, Kew Gardens, and all BBC references are from the BBC Written Archives Centre (BBCWAC) at Caversham.[7]

Interviews provided the second rich primary source of information. When reading archival documents it is crucial to locate that person and to understand their position in order to do justice to their views. We have spoken with FCO officials and specialists who had actually signed the documents during the 1970s, and are particularly grateful to Sir John Leahy and the late Chris Rundle who generously offered their guidance and read some of the relevant chapters with their sharp critical eyes.

Another source of original information was a Witness Seminar on *The BBC and the Iranian Revolution* organized by the Centre for Media and Film Studies at SOAS in March 2010.[8] The seminar heard several firsthand accounts of exceptional personalities who had either been directly involved in or personally witnessed the tension between the FCO, the BBC Persian Service and the Shah of Iran during the Iranian Revolution of 1979. Professor Fred Halliday, who as a young researcher had travelled to Tehran during the revolution of 1979, gave his last public analysis of the Iranian Revolution before his untimely death in April 2010. Lord David Owen, who had been the British Foreign Secretary, spoke of his meetings with the Shah of Iran and the mounting tension between the British government and the BBC over the two years leading to the revolution. Andrew Whitley, the BBC correspondent in Tehran during the Iranian Revolution, Chris Rundle of the FCO who oversaw many of the reviews of the BBC, and Mark Dodd, head of the BBC's Eastern Service, were amongst other speakers at the seminar. We draw on their witness accounts and the discussions and debates in that seminar.

Interviews and analysis were offered by the former Member of Parliament, Ahmad Salamatian; the historian of Iran's labour movement, Khosrow Shakeri; the founder of the National Democratic Front, Hedayat Matin Daftari; the first president of the Islamic Republic, Abolhassan Banisadr; and the Shah's minister of information, the late Darioush Homayoun. Each provided us with unique insights, particularly into the last three months of the Iranian Revolution and on Ayatollah Khomeini's political communication from France.

Current staff at the BBC including Behrouz Afagh, Andres Ilves, Sadeq Saba, Pooneh Ghodousi, Roxanna Shahpour, Leyla Khodabakshi and some of the former BBC Persian Service staff such as Lotfali Khonji, Shadab Vajdi, Sharon Tabari, Solmaz Dabiri, Shahryard Radpoor, Ali Asghar Ramezanpoor generously shared their insights. The former head and deputy head of the BBC Eastern Service, William Crawley and David Page, and the former BBC heads of the Persian and Pashto Services, Baqer Moin and Gordon Adam, commented on relevant chapters and shared their experience of and perceptions about the inner workings of the relations between the FCO and the BBC.

We would like to thank all those who spoke with us and gave so generously of their time and thoughts, although they hold no responsibility for the arguments and opinions put forward here.

BBC staff impressed us throughout the project with their openness and responsiveness. We recognize the great sacrifices often made by those who have and continue to work for the Persian services, then and now, and wish them well.

1

From Propaganda to Public Diplomacy: The Changing Paradigms

Human history is in many ways a history of differing forms of communication, from warlike aggression to trading relations. New technologies have always played a key role in enabling different kinds of communicative patterns. The advent of print revolutionized how people lived, first in Europe and then spreading across the world. The creation of the telegraph aided the development of train schedules and the linking of continents, providing the infrastructure for international news agencies such as Havas and Reuters to produce shared news stories for national newspapers by the mid-nineteenth century.

It was the development of radio in the 1920s that truly began to link national audiences together. The early choices about ownership and control of radio also set patterns that endure to this day. The revolutionary Russians invested heavily in radio development under the centralized People's Commissariat for Posts and Telegraphs (PCPT), establishing a model for the state control of broadcasting that still exists in many countries. The US chose a privately owned and advertising-funded path of commercial radio development in its 1927 Radio Act. Britain trod a third path.

The establishment of the BBC

The beginnings of broadcasting in Britain came in the early 1920s. The British Broadcasting Company was established as a commercial entity in 1922 by a UK electro-technical industry consortium that included Marconi, Metropolitan Vickers, GEC, British Thomson Houston, Western Electric and the Radio Communication Company. The new company built a national network of radio transmitters in London, Manchester and Birmingham as the basis for a UK-wide broadcasting service. It was replaced by the British Broadcasting Corporation in 1927 under the leadership of Director-General John Reith (1889–1971), who reportedly boasted that the organization 'has never attempted to give the public what it wants. It gives the public what it ought to have.'[1] He famously defined its ongoing ethos as one of 'public service' broadcasting, of an independent British broadcaster able to educate, inform and entertain the whole nation, free from political interference and commercial pressure. The innovation of a Post Office licence fee of ten shillings (currently worth around 50 pence), of which half went to the BBC, ensured that the BBC was not financially dependent on the government of the day nor on advertising revenue. The BBC remains funded by the licence fee which is transferred via Parliament to the BBC. In December 2010 the annual fee was set at £145.50 for up to 15 sets, while a black-and-white TV licence was £49.

However, the World Service model of financing was very different again. We need to tell a different story.

The Empire Service

On 19 December 1932, the BBC set up a short-wave Empire Service that was intended to address English-speaking diasporas, the embodied remnants of empire strewn around the world. It was built around new short-wave radio technology that allowed signals to be broadcast over vast distances. It could be called a practice of 'communicating with ourselves abroad', aimed at strengthening British diasporic ties with the homeland and building a sense of dispersed community. The BBC's director-general John Reith was wonderfully unenthusiastic to begin with, famously warning in early broadcasts: 'Don't expect too much in the early days; for some time we shall transmit comparatively simple programmes, to give the best chance of intelligible reception and provide evidence as to the type of material most suitable for the service in each zone. The programmes will neither be very interesting nor very good.'[2] Yet the broadcasts received praise, and were further boosted by the support of the first ever Christmas message from King George V to the Empire a few days later. The BBC Empire Service went on air to five world time zones on its first day, with the 'Australasian Zone' the first to receive the broadcast that started with what became its well-known signature phrase: 'This is London calling.'[3]

World War II changed everything. Britain was in a state of total war with every resource focused on winning the battle against the Axis powers. At first, the BBC's role was somewhat uncertain. The BBC Archive timeline recounts the story of the first days thus:

> Managers at the fledgling corporation debated whether the BBC should report the conflict objectively – or contribute to the war effort by broadcasting morale boosting propaganda. By the autumn of 1940, Britain was suffering almost nightly bombardment from German planes. On 15 October a delayed action bomb hit Broadcasting House in London. It landed in the music library at 2010 GMT and exploded 52 minutes later, killing seven people. Listeners to the Nine o'clock news heard the announcer pause, and then continue reading.[4]

The BBC reinvented itself during World War II, more than doubling in size and adopting a new culture and outlook. The biggest expansion came early in 1940–1, ahead of American involvement in the war, when the outlook for Britain was bleakest. The Churchill government asked the BBC to increase its overseas effort threefold. A special service for North America was introduced, offering entertainment as well as news of the British struggle. There were services in every major European language and services were introduced for the Soviet Union, India, Japan and more. Suddenly the BBC was radio broadcasting in eight languages including English, in recognition of the need to communicate to others in their countries of origin; this was the formal start of organized and publicly funded international communication to foreign audiences. The war proved to be a tough test of the BBC's independence. At times the government and the military wanted to use the BBC to counter crude propaganda from the Nazis and the Italians, and there was even talk in Westminster of taking over the BBC. So it was wartime necessity that saw a huge expansion of the international remit of the service, now renamed the Overseas Service, with coverage in over 40 different languages by the end of the war. A dedicated BBC European Service was added in 1941. Known administratively as the External Services of the BBC, these were financed not from the domestic licence fee but from government grant-in-aid out of the Foreign Office budget. Also in 1941, its activities became centred in Bush House where it remained until its move to New Broadcasting House in 2012. The service was renamed the BBC World Service in 1965.

While the BBC World Service is considered to function in 'the national interest', it has always striven to remain editorially independent of its paymaster, the Foreign Office. Thus it has functioned with a deep and intriguing tension at the heart of its activities. The World Service has been subject to the changing priorities and concerns of British foreign policy. However, the language services themselves have always argued for and have come to operate under the sign of impartiality and distance from direct government influence, which is the rubric of the BBC. The exploration of this tension, the inelegant dance between financial control versus editorial independence, is one of the core strands of this book.

The Middle East was central to the early expansion of the service, revealing early foreign-policy concerns. BBC Arabic began broadcasting in January 1938, the first foreign-language transmission. Persian-language broadcasting was established in December 1940, organized into a separate department of Near East Services along with Turkish-language broadcasting. For a decade after World War II, the BBC World Service could be said to have enjoyed 'radio superiority' in the region, based on the continuity and experience of its personnel, their long residencies and their knowledge of the cultures, and had built up regular listenerships.

The BBC Arabic Service's main competition in the late 1940s was from the Near East Arab Broadcasting station, Sharq al-Adna, which operated as a supposedly independent commercial station from Palestine, relocating to Cyprus in 1948. Actually, it was operated by the FCO in secret in order to present British polices from a standpoint sympathetic to Arab audiences. It was very popular but more propagandist than the BBC and listened to in Middle Eastern coffee shops. It was likened to the *Daily Mail*, which had a large circulation but still did not rival *The Times*. The BBC itself was really targeting the influential intelligentsia in the region, not the so-called 'Arab street'. It brought in Arab literary and cultural figures such as Taha Hussein and in 1944 was called 'the university of modern times' by an enthusiastic listener.[5] Of course, both of these channels competed for audience attention with Gamal Abdel Nasser's *Voice of the Arabs* (*Sawt al-Arab*) that broadcast on Cairo Radio from 1952 and became the main voice of the popular revolution. Strongly anti-colonial and pan-Arabist, it helped Nasser's leadership of the Arab nationalist movement and his move into the Egyptian presidency.

By the time of the Suez Crisis, BBC Arabic was broadcasting for over 30 hours per week, compared with French radio's three hours per day, Radio Moscow's one hour and Voice of America (VOA)'s three hours, which was increased to six in November 1956 in response to the political instability growing in the region as a result of the crisis. So Britain was clearly not alone in investing in international radio broadcasting to reach foreign audiences and shape public opinion inside other countries.

As the Middle East was central to the development of foreign-language radio broadcasting in the 1940s, so it was also the first region in the roll-out of World Service television, which was launched in March 2008, broadcasting first in Arabic.[6] Persian was the second language service to move into television; this is explored in detail in the last chapter. The move into television was paid for by the elimination of a number of radio language services to countries then deemed to be on the road to democracy and no longer in need of the BBC's content. So assessments of political need and British government priorities have directed the flow of FCO funds, but the governmental hand that made the payments could not directly determine the content.

Our analysis of archived documents reveals the tussle between the two interests – British government priorities and BBC editorial independence – from the beginning, even at times of war. BBC's audience research has also repeatedly proved that the greatest single factor contributing to whatever success BBC foreign broadcasts have achieved is the integrity of the news content. The BBC's journalism for international audiences 'should share the same values as its journalism for UK audiences: accuracy, impartiality and independence.'[7] As a result, the BBC claims that 'levels of trust among BBC World Service audiences remain very high. And the long tradition of global audiences turning to the BBC for trustworthy news in times of crisis continues strongly.'[8]

The development of international radio was perhaps the critical moment when media institutions began to conceive of and develop forms of communication that addressed foreign audiences, even if this is now supplemented with television and the internet. So the actual practices of international communication have prefigured the various academic attempts to conceptualize and define these practices. There is growing competition to name this new type of communication, usually as forms of emerging 'public diplomacy', and its translation into policy tools of international diplomacy, often in a rather weakly conceptualized manner. We will now look briefly at these rhetorics as developed within the Western academy. Later, we explore how this language has been adopted by the Islamic Republic.

A brief history of 'public diplomacy' and 'soft power'

In any discussion of this subject, we are confronted by a semantic soup of terms used to define international communication, from the usually pejorative 'propaganda' – which other countries practice – to the more anodyne 'public diplomacy' which 'we' do, and from psychological warfare to 'soft power' and nation-branding.

Public diplomacy as a distinct mode of foreign policy was developed as countries sought to communicate directly with overseas publics, and its modes have included a mix of cultural programmes, educational exchanges and mediated communications, often targeting educated elites. The actual coinage of the term is most often connected to Edmund Gullion, when he established the Edward R. Murrow Center of Public Diplomacy in 1965. As the University of Southern California website clearly notes, the term 'public diplomacy was developed partly to distance overseas governmental information activities from the term *propaganda*, which had acquired pejorative connotations'.[9] Hans N. Tuch describes the purpose of public diplomacy as a 'government's process of communicating with foreign publics in an attempt to bring about understanding for its nation's ideas and ideals, its institutions and cultures, as well as its national goals and current policies'.[10]

The scholarly field of public diplomacy is strongly American in origin, and even the emergence of what is called 'new public diplomacy' developed there after the September 2011 attacks. Then the Bush administration oversaw the creation of the Office of Global Communications to coordinate the global public relations efforts of the US government through a variety of platforms such as advertisements, websites, radio programmes and news stories. US public diplomacy efforts targeting the Middle East were intensified and greatly expanded under the direction of former advertising executive Charlotte Beers who headed the State Department efforts.[11]

'New public diplomacy' was defined more broadly than activity unique to sovereign states. It reflected the changing face of international relations as a range of non-state actors gained a role in world politics and it recognized that diverse supranational organizations, non-governmental organizations and corporations now communicate directly with foreign publics and thereby develop and promote public diplomacy policies, and practices of their own. Thus the epoch of state-centric foreign relations has been replaced by a more complex global environment that is composed of multiple actors and networks who are elaborating new issues and concerns. To quote Pamment:

> [T]he new public diplomacy (PD) is a major paradigm shift in international political communication. Globalization and a new media landscape challenge traditional foreign ministry 'gatekeeper' structures, and foreign ministries can no longer lay claim to being sole or dominant actors in communicating foreign policy. This demands new ways of elucidating foreign policy to a range of nongovernmental international actors, and new ways of evaluating the influence of these communicative efforts.[12]

Many now see public diplomacy as merely a form of international public relations. As Wang and Chang[13] argue, public diplomacy and public relations both seek to reach out to target publics with the goal of maintaining and managing images, and the two practices share a great deal of strategic and tactical commonalities.

Beers herself compared public diplomacy efforts to marketing, drawing out the importance of achieving the desired perceptual, attitudinal and behavioural change in the target audience. She suggested that public diplomacy in the Middle East needed to have clear and simple messages, include emotions in the messages, and build on the basic principles of persuasion. US tactical public relations activities after 9/11 included a range of print and electronic pamphlets with titles such as *The Network of Terrorism, Iraq: From Fear to Freedom* and *Voices of Freedom*; an Arabic youth magazine; and an 18-minute documentary entitled *Rebuilding Afghanistan*.[14] Other tactical public diplomacy tools include old and new US international broadcasting operations such as the Voice of America, Worldnet Television and Film Service, Radio/TV Marti, Radio Free Europe/Radio Liberty, Radio Free Asia, Radio Sawa and Radio Farda.[15]

So the new public diplomacy is no longer confined to messaging, promotion campaigns or even direct governmental contacts with foreign publics serving foreign-policy purposes. The focus now includes building relationships with civil-society actors in other countries and facilitating networks between non-governmental parties at home and abroad. Thus current UK government policy is aimed at promoting such cross-border networks, recognizing that unselective government control can undercut the credibility that such networks are designed to engender. The evolution of public diplomacy from one-way communications to a two-way dialogue supposedly treats publics as co-creators of meaning and communication.

This expanded idea of 'new public diplomacy' in both theory and practice clearly targets much wider audiences than only the educated elites and includes a wider range of techniques. A major guru behind such thinking is Joseph Nye with his concept of soft power, defined as 'the ability to get what you want through attraction rather than coercion or payments'.[16] Defined thus, the concept has no sense of any transnational reach and evokes older Marxist notions of the 'dominant ideology' or Antonio Gramsci's notion of 'cultural hegemony', albeit that this critical tradition thought negatively about such practices whereas Nye is a positive advocate for them.

The critical media scholar Herb Schiller[17] argued that soft power was a euphemism for what he called 'cultural imperialism' and we will see later how that argument has been taken up by strong states. But Nye also recognized that 'a communications strategy cannot work if it cuts against the grain of policy. Actions speak louder than words. All too often, policymakers treat public diplomacy as a bandage that can be applied after damage is done by other instruments.'[18] He cites the Chinese attempt to enhance its soft power by successfully staging the 2008 Olympics while simultaneously cracking down in Tibet and arresting human rights lawyers, thereby undercutting any gains.[19] Equally, the power of Hollywood imagery might be tempered by US military drone strikes or the power of the BBC by UK government renditions.

Evidently, the use of power in a global information age will include a soft dimension of attraction as well as the hard dimensions of coercion and payment, now often called by another neologism, 'smart power'. This was defined, in a 2007 report on smart power by the Centre for Strategic and International Studies, co-chaired by Nye and Richard Armitage, as recognizing the need to use various forms of power, as and when necessary. As they put it, smart power recognizes 'the necessity of a strong military, but also invests heavily in alliances, partnerships, and institutions of all levels to expand American influence and establish legitimacy of American action'.[20]

Nye argues that the current struggle against transnational terrorism, a term he doesn't define, is a struggle over winning hearts and minds, and over-reliance on hard power alone is not the path to success:

> Public diplomacy is an important tool in the arsenal of smart power, but smart public diplomacy requires an understanding of credibility, self-criticism, and the role of civil society in generating soft power. If it degenerates into propaganda, public diplomacy not only fails to convince, but can undercut soft power. Instead, it must remain a two-way process, because soft power depends, first and foremost, upon understanding the minds of others.[21]

British coinages and uses

While less developed as an academic field in Britain, the rhetoric of 'public diplomacy' is increasingly evident in British foreign policy speak. It took on new focus and urgency after the 9/11 attacks and the war with Iraq; thus, once again, issues relating to the Middle East are broadly the trigger for new thinking and policy orientations. A key text is the 2002 report *Public Diplomacy*, by Leonard, Stead and Smewing, that builds on the earlier draft document entitled *Going Public*. It was produced by the Foreign Policy Centre, an independent think-tank launched by then Prime Minister Tony Blair and his former Foreign Secretary Robin Cook 'to examine the impact of globalisation on foreign and domestic policy'. Leonard *et al.* argued that while governments now recognized the importance of this new type of diplomacy, they did not allocate sufficient funds to promote it adequately; that more attention needed to be paid to the way that foreign audiences would receive stories, which was best done 'not through embassies on the ground, but by working through foreign correspondents in your own capital';[22] and that governments needed to learn a new form of communication, 'building long-term relationships and understanding target groups rather than delivering one-way messages'.[23]

Over the past decade, successive governments have been endlessly rearranging the pieces involved to form a serious policy. In 2002, after the Wilton Review recommended greater coordination, the Public Diplomacy Strategy Board was established by the Blair government to coordinate all government work in 'communicating and building relations with publics around the world'. This acknowledged the range of organizations then involved in such work and brought together the work of the FCO, the British Council, the British Tourist Authority and UK Trade and Investment. A common strategy was agreed and its emerging definition of public diplomacy was:

> work which aims at influencing in a positive way, including through the creation of relationships and partnerships, the perceptions of individuals and organisations overseas about the UK and their engagement with the UK, in support of HMG's overseas objectives.[24]

The BBC World Service and the British Council are the two principal government-funded bodies involved in public diplomacy activity. In 2004–5, they received £225 million and £172 million of grant-in-aid respectively. The Foreign Office's public diplomacy expenditure in 2004–5 (excluding British Council, World Service and Chevening scholarship funding) was around £165 million, while the total UK grant-funded public diplomacy expenditure in 2005–6 was £617 million. Such figures support Leonard's notion that public diplomacy activity in Britain has comparatively large goals and little resource.

A subsequent review, undertaken by Lord Carter in December 2004 and reporting in December 2005, sought a further refinement of public diplomacy. It argued that this should no longer be defined simply in terms of creating positive perceptions, but as:

> work aiming to inform and engage individuals and organizations overseas, in order to improve understanding of and influence for the United Kingdom in a manner consistent with governmental medium and long term goals.[25]

Leonard and Small write:

> [W]e now face a more complex set of challenges. In broad terms, the UK now confronts two major public diplomacy goals: advocacy – the presentation of the UK and its policies in ways that are genuinely convincing and attractive to international audiences; and trust-building – the creation of a climate of mutual respect, understanding and trust, which permits and anticipates disagreement[…] much clearer articulation of public diplomacy and cultural relations objectives. As well as showcasing Britain as a modern and innovative country, such a strategy will demonstrate that Britain is a principled power which believes in international law, global development, and European unity.[26]

Following the Carter Review, the Public Diplomacy Board was set up in April 2006 along with the Public Diplomacy Partners Group, replacing the Public Diplomacy Strategy Board. This now included the FCO and British Council, while the BBC World Service enjoyed observer status in recognition of its editorial independence.

In 2006, the secretary of state for foreign and commonwealth affairs, Jack Straw, acknowledged that the Carter Review was right to recognize the BBC World Service's unique contribution to the UK's public diplomacy 'as a world class international broadcaster and to understand the significance of its editorial independence to its reputation and ability to deliver an unbiased trustworthy news service'.[27] He further concluded that making decisions on priority markets and new investment in a manner consistent with governmental medium- to long-term goals, in consultation with the FCO, should not be detrimental to the BBC World Service's editorial impartiality; recommended regular reviews of the BBC World Service to ensure that resources were being utilized to achieve a maximum impact, giving overall audience figures; and considered that there remain considerable advantages for the BBC World Service remaining structurally bound into the overall FCO operation: 'We conclude that the ringfenced funding for the BBC World Service and the British Council should remain in place.'[28]

So the FCO remained the controller of the purse strings, deciding on markets and investments, while the editorial impartiality of the BBC World Service remained intact. Such a relationship is, of course, an interesting challenge to the classic notion of media ownership and control, whereby the money paid seems to also determine the output. The British debate hinges upon a very different assumption, that the 'impartiality' of the BBC World Service must be maintained as its major source of value, even while funding for current services and new initiatives remains with the FCO. If this is hard for media scholars and the British public to understand, how much harder must it be for foreign governments and audiences.

In October 2009, the then Labour government proposed yet another renaming and change of remit. The FCO decided to replace the Public Diplomacy Board with a new Strategic

Communications and Public Diplomacy Forum, to meet twice a year and be chaired directly by the Foreign Secretary. This would be supported by a Public Diplomacy Partners Group which would meet at a lower level, under FCO chairmanship, roughly every six weeks, to focus on cross-cutting themes and events. The FCO minister with responsibility for public diplomacy would now focus on ministerial supervision of the relationship between the FCO and its 'directly funded partners', primarily the British Council and BBC World Service, these new arrangements recognizing 'the more central place that public diplomacy is taking in the FCO's work'.[29]

The Coalition government that came to power in May 2010 has not yet made a formal declaration of its policy in relation to public diplomacy. The new Foreign Secretary, Rt Hon William Hague MP, vaguely referred to the concept of public diplomacy in his first policy speech, delivered at the FCO on 1 July 2010:

> [I]f the increasingly multipolar world already means that we have more governments to influence and that we must become more active, the ever accelerating development of human networks means that we have to use many more channels to do so, seeking to carry our arguments in courts of public opinion around the world as well as around international negotiating tables. [...] In my mind, such communication will become all the more important over time and as we conduct our diplomacy across the world we overlook international opinion at our peril, and while we cannot possibly hope to dominate the global airwaves we must try ever harder to get our message across.[30]

But the airwaves are not the only space for international communications. Increasingly, public diplomacy initiatives have become digital and moved onto the internet.[31]

The FCO, like many other diplomatic services, has developed a substantial 'digital diplomacy' initiative in recent years.[32] A more web-savvy FCO has diplomats blogging and tweeting away as they make Britain's case in an informal way with audiences around the world. The FCO has experimented with intensive online campaigns, notably its Nuclear 2010 campaign in support of UK objectives for the review of the non-proliferation treaty, the campaign to secure the release of Aung San Suu Kyi, and the campaign to shape global opinion during the London G20 summit. The FCO has put in place various kinds of internet outreach to Iran and the recent ambassador to Tehran (2009–11), Simon Gass, was an active tweeter while in office.

Of course, the BBC World Service has been actively online for many years, seeing online activity as a significant complement to radio and television broadcasting and a powerful tool for building trust in interaction with foreign audiences, particularly with diasporic populations.[33] The Persian online site was blocked in January 2006 and has only been accessible by hacking or using filter-blocking since then.

Perhaps the biggest shake-up to the BBC World Service in its history was announced by the Coalition in early 2011. As part of the Coalition's plans to reduce the deficit, the BBC World Service had to bear some shrinkage.[34] It was to move from its long-standing home in Bush House to be physically integrated with the rest of the BBC in new premises at New Broadcasting House, a move carried out in 2012. More significant still, BBC World Service funding is to be taken from the FCO and transferred to general television licence fee funding in April 2014. This implies a loss of 650 posts by 2014, as well as a reduction in audiences by more than 30 million from the current weekly audience of 180 million. The changes have been approved by the BBC Trust, the BBC Executive and, in relation to closure of services, the secretary of state for foreign and commonwealth affairs, William Hague, as his approval is required under the terms of the BBC's agreement with the FCO. Whether and how this will impact on the function of the World Service remains to be seen.[35] One real danger is that in a period of greater austerity, the British viewing public may well wonder why they are paying for foreign broadcasting over improved domestic programming – an argument that will take much finesse to explain. The other issue is whether this significant shift, not only in funding but

also in location within the organization, and change of controlling structure, will be recognized and understood by foreign
governments such as that in Iran.

The main point of this brief review of changes in the focus
and organization of public diplomacy in Britain is to show how
the fate of the BBC World Service has been linked to changes
in political priorities and organizational arrangements by successive governments. So the BBC World Service has been buffeted
by political exigencies while its essential argument, that it must
remain editorially free of government intervention and impartial, has been increasingly accepted by British governments as the
badge of trust for international audiences.

Iranian coinages

While Iranian political discourses do not function in the register
of public diplomacy, the growth of international broadcasting
from Iran and its political strategies show an acute perception
of international communication and the need for appropriate
political rhetorics. Indeed, the Iranian political establishment has
often had a good ear for new coinages in Western rhetoric and
sometimes uses that very language against the West.

Khomeini led the 1979 popular revolution against the
Pahlavi dynasty but also against foreign interference in Iranian
politics, a feature of its twentieth-century history, including
most prominently the 1953 US/British coup that overthrew the
democratically elected government of Mossadeq and returned
Mohammad Reza Pahlavi to power. Opposition to the twin
enemies of imperialism and Zionism and steadfastness against
'bullying and arrogant powers' are themes that continue to run
through the politics of the Islamic Republic. The taking over
of the US Embassy in 1979 and the extended hostage crisis
has meant that the Islamic Republic has never enjoyed direct
diplomatic relations with the US. This has contributed to the
vacillation of Iranian foreign policy as to which is the bigger

threat – the US or Britain – and the emergence of Britain as the main protagonist in 'soft war', issues that will be addressed in subsequent chapters.

The notion of cultural imperialism, of the negative effects of Western popular culture on Islamic tradition, was also promulgated by the Islamic Republic. This reached an apex during the Rushdie affair in 1989 when Khomeini declared a fatwa against the author. From early on after the revolution, internal dissenters were labelled as foreign agitators, proxies for the US and its allies.[36] A more constructive period of potential engagement with the West seemed to emerge under the presidency of Mohammad Khatami (1997–2005) with his notion of the 'dialogue of civilizations'. This clearly played with and gave a more positive spin to the notion of the 'clash of civilizations', Samuel Huntington's (1993) assessment that the world was increasingly divided into religious cultures that did not understand each other.[37] A number of conferences were organized under Khatami's rubric; the UN even proclaimed 2001 as the year of dialogue of civilizations. But the conservative forces were also active. As Adelkhah writes:

> hardliners, with the help of the intelligence-military complex, [...] step[ped] up measures to counter-attack soft threats. These included efforts to defend IRGC political activities from reformist critiques. When the 1999 student uprising challenged the regime's tight grip over the press and the imprisonment of a number of reformists, the discourse of coup became an everyday staple of the hardliners' media.[38]

And then came the 11 September 2001 attacks on American soil. Many Iranians flooded onto the streets of Tehran with candles in memory of those who died and there was no evidence to link the Islamic Republic to the event. Yet President Bush claimed that Iran was linked to al Qaeda and thus implicated in the new 'war against terror', and considered Iran to be part of a new 'axis of evil'. The Islamic Republic responded with its own notion of an 'axis of resistance' to US imperialism, especially focusing on support for Palestinian resistance.

24   Persian Service

During the period of Khatami's presidency (1997–2005), non-governmental organizations tried to establish themselves under Khatami and the idea of an independent 'civil society' ('*jameh madani*') began to develop. But under Ahmadinejad's presidency from 2005 on, the state took over that rhetoric, developing state-supported NGOs inside Iran and accusing some diaspora Iranians such as Ramin Jahanbeglou and Haleh Esfandiari in 2006–7 of supporting a 'velvet revolution' ('*enghelab-e makhmali*') against the Islamic Republic.

One definition of such a process of 'soft topple' was developed by Hamid Mowlana, once Professor of International Communication at American University, Washington, DC, but latterly a political advisor to Ahmadinejad. Mowlana defines it as:

> the overthrowing of a system or a government in a non-military way, by provoking the people to riot and by using psychological, destructive propaganda and deceptive methods using the media and information and communication tools. A velvet revolution takes place by coordinating domestic and foreign assistance.[39]

He made comparisons with the processes of political change, generally considered to be coup d'états, in Ukraine, Kyrgyzstan, Georgia and Serbia and the similarities with the post-election politics of 2009.

So, both at the same time, the regime has playfully subverted Western discourses to suit its politics, as well as displaying an increasingly adversarial tone toward internal dissidents and Western powers alike.

The latest change of political language has been the transformation of Joseph Nye's concept of 'soft power' into one of 'soft war' ('*jang-e narm*'). The notion of 'soft war' has been articulated by Ayatollah Khamenei, although he does not seem to be the originator of the concept; indeed, its genealogy is hard to precisely determine. Notions of 'soft war', 'soft warriors', 'soft threat' and other such constructions were already in circulation by 2007. Mohammad Baqer Zolqadr, deputy interior minister for security and law enforcement, argued that 'the main policy of America is "soft threat" by creating instability and crisis inside Iran, and exacerbating ethnic and religious fault lines'. He said that 'in the context of its soft threat, America uses newspapers and NGOs by copying programmes of the former Soviet Union, and some [domestic] newspapers, in line with the aims of enemies, are carrying out their duties quite well'.[40] Minister of culture and Islamic guidance, Mohammad-Hossein Safar-Harandi, said at the opening of a cultural centre in the north of Iran that: 'Nowadays, soft war is on the super powers agenda and this war is fighting in cultural fields.' He referred to the limitations of military power, saying: 'Super powers' experiences in the recent decades have led them to extend influence in countries where the military conflict is not the only choice.' And he added that Iran was 'armed with soft war special weapons and the soldiers of such a war are intellectuals and media...so places like this are our barracks to fight against enemies'.[41]

By early 2009, the notion of 'soft war' was clearly in circulation. But its focus was still shifting. In an article by Hamid Omidi headlined 'The arena of two rivals', published by the conservative newspaper *Keyhan* on 22 February 2009, the focus was clearly the US. The US was said to have been unsuccessful in its 'warmongering and dominating plans' and therefore, the article said, the Republicans and neo-Conservatives in the Bush government had launched 'the soft war' in their confrontation with Iran many years ago; but the author considers that the same strategy was likely to be followed by Obama's Democrats. Omidi names Karen Hughes, Bush's undersecretary of state for public diplomacy, as key to 'the soft war's command room' with 'news and propaganda bombardment of Iran, a very small part of these plans'. Omidi writes:

> Soft war which has now been launched against the system of the Islamic Republic of Iran as a big project is identified by characteristics such as the organization of civil dissatisfaction, creation of economic disorganization, help towards the establishment of

NGOs on a wide scale with the objective of deliberately or unintentionally exploiting them along the path of implementation of overthrowing plans, media wars, psychological operations for making the country's executive apparatus appear ineffective and finally the important characteristic of cultural NATO.[42]

We just note briefly the use of another fascinating coinage, 'cultural NATO', as part of the rhetorical assemblage that makes up the idea of 'soft war'. This coinage had been in circulation at least since August 2007, when Ali Sa'idi, Ayatollah Khamenei's representative in the Iranian Revolutionary Guard Corps (IRGC), described it as a weapon in asymmetrical combat. Sa'idi was reiterating a recent speech by Khamenei, arguing that:

> the enemy's field of activity comprises the whole country and if we look closer, it comprises the whole geography of the Islamic world. According to the leader's guidelines on how to recognize vulnerability, we have to identify three processes; the first is cultural invasion which he proposed in previous years, the second was cultural ambush and the third is the enemies' attempts to change NATO's function from military to cultural.

Sa'idi's reasoning for this shift is worth quoting at length:

> because of an awakening in the Islamic world and the Islamic Republic's guiding power within the region and the Islamic countries, they felt seriously threatened by the power of Islam and they put two debates into practice. In the first stage, they started military operations after the 9/11 event and they entered the region with the aim of blockading Iran from the East and the West and they first conquered Afghanistan and then Iraq in order to isolate Iran. However, they also started their cultural work alongside the military one; from strengthening Salman Rushdie who heaped the greatest insults on the Prophet of Islam to supporting journalistic efforts which started in Denmark and involved sacrilegious caricatures and George Bush's speeches about the crusades which in effect brought to mind the war between Islam and Christianity in the Middle Ages and they did

not even hesitate to involve the Pope in this issue…I believe that NATO's cultural function is considerably more dangerous than its military one and we only realise this point when we compare the two functions. Military function is essentially more costly and involves many casualties whereas such a thing does not apply to the cultural function. Its costs are low and its coverage is extensive.[43]

Thus it is evident that such ideas were gaining traction over a number of years, developed by and supporting the political conservatives, since the best defence against such cultural attacks was seen to be the strengthening of Islamic institutions and a greater spirituality.[44] Arguments about preparing the Iranian people and developing their political knowledge to foil 'cultural onslaught' or cultural invasion were often repeated, especially by the IRGC, while the Basij (a volunteer militia subordinate to the command of the IRGC) was seen as a key organization in implementing such a process.

Nonetheless, the main thrust for the military strategic development of 'soft war' seems to have been triggered by the popular uprising against the fraudulent presidential election result of June 2009 and the massive global media interest in the 'Green Movement' that developed. The details of the political dynamics of June 2009 and the specific attacks on BBC PTV are elaborated in Chapter 6. Here, we simply continue to try to unravel the development of the rhetoric of 'soft war'.

In an interview in November 2009 with Ali Mohammad Na'ini, then deputy head of the Basij militia for cultural and social affairs, the interviewer himself acknowledged the soup of terms in current circulation in Iran:

'Cultural attack', 'cultural onslaught', 'cultural NATO', 'soft threats' and more recently 'soft war' are some of the terms that have been often used by the experts and the members of the elite. These terms provide some strong interpretations and proven evaluations of the cultural and social conditions and circumstances of the country.[45]

But the interview settles down into an interrogation of the idea of 'soft war', which Na'ini elaborated thus:

> The main aim behind the Soft War is to force the system to disintegrate from within in view of its values, beliefs, its main fundamental characteristics, and its identity. Any system, especially a system that is based on certain beliefs and values, owes its identity and its existence to those beliefs and values. It is based on the models and principles on the basis of which it continues its political, social and economic life [...] If the identity or the fundamental beliefs and values and the main model of a revolution in different social, political, cultural and economic fields are challenged by non-military means the adherence of the society to that system would be challenged.[46]

It is important to note that in terms of communications theory this sounds remarkably like the 'hypodermic needle' model of direct effects; Na'ini never stops to ask why 'adherence of the society' would be so easily challenged or an external voice so powerful.

Both Khamenei and General Mohammed Ali Jafari, the IRGC Commander, have explicitly accused Western states and non-governmental groups of conducting 'soft war' to undermine the Islamic Republic, the former saying: 'Today, the main priority of the country is to confront [the enemy's] soft warfare which is aimed at creating doubt, discord and pessimism among the masses of the people.'[47] By August 2012, Jafari was saying that this was the biggest threat that Iran currently faced.[48]

An article in *Resalat*, a conservative newspaper, mentioned both Song Tzu's [sic] *Art of War* (estimated to have been written around 400 BCE) and Mu'awiya, the seventh-century caliph of Damascus, in its attempt to write a genealogy of the concept, ending with:

> if we were to present a definition of soft war one could define this as 'any move possibly presented as a preliminary to military war and targeting the opposite side's morale'. All plans made in this framework are thus defined as soft war.[49]

It was without a doubt the establishment of BBC PTV in January 2009, followed by its prominent role in covering the aftermath of the 2009 presidential election, that made the BBC become the central opponent in the regime's development of its 'soft war' strategy. Further detail of the dynamics of 2009 are provided in Chapter 6.

The conservative website, *Alef*, owned by the Majlis deputy Ahmad Tavakoli (who was once close to the mayor of Tehran, Mohammad Bagher Ghalibaf, himself a former general in the IRGC), defines soft war as:

> an alternative for classic and military-based wars between hostile countries and governments. The recent example of the soft war was the situation after the presidential elections. The soft war has all the elements of a war to defeat the enemy. Satellites, anti-revolution websites, resolutions and intimidating political analysis are the enemy's tools. The defensive approaches to these attacks include satellites, pro-revolution sites and even technical defense like jamming the enemy's satellite and stopping the intimidating websites from spreading lies.[50]

This definition tries to establish a precise starting point with the disputed election and its communications tools and also outlines the 'defensive' measures that the regime is undertaking.

From this brief review of the somewhat confused development of the idea of 'soft war', it is evident that Iranian analysts have a keen ear for the nuances of Western foreign policy rhetoric and are very able to turn it to their advantage. The above quotations come from political and religious figures, members of the IRGC and journalists, suggesting a concerted effort to promulgate such concepts in support of a strategic shift in policy. In line with the continual revolutionary logic that internal dissidence has external origins, 'soft war' became a military strategic plan elaborated by Major General Mohammad Ali Jafari, the commander of the IRGC. So the notion of 'soft war' has become a key plank of the foreign policy, especially the military strategy, of the Islamic Republic.[51] It is also easy to see from such rhetoric how investment in international broadcasting and the development of numerous foreign-language channels became an important part of the Islamic Republic's expansion of its state broadcasting corporation, details about which we give in Chapter 6.

It is not only within Western countries that arguments about the significance of 'public diplomacy' have been staged. Indeed, the global airwaves are now full – if not saturated – with broadcast signals in numerous languages, a veritable electronic Tower of Babel. What became particularly fascinating about the Iranian position was the contradictory position it seemed to manifest, allowing for the legitimacy of its international broadcasting but not that of other actors. The tense stand-off with BBC PTV is also addressed in Chapter 6.

We have not tried to provide the definitive or most critical overview of these changing discourses, either in the West or inside Iran; both are still badly needed. The point is to show the changing frameworks within which the role of the BBC World Service has been defined, and to explore the take-up of such rhetorics elsewhere, especially inside the Islamic Republic. Our argument is that the actual practices and the discourses around these practices were and are highly political. One of the conceptual problems of defining a field in such an all-encompassing manner is that many activities that have intentionally little to do with a national policy can come to be seen both by national players and by external ones as part and parcel of such a national policy. That is to say that independent actors, perhaps small NGOs, can be seen as coopted by the larger national framework and seen as fifth-columnists by foreign powers. It is little wonder that the BBC World Service – from its early radio activity, and later its television broadcasting – became embroiled in such bitter controversy.

2

The Establishment of
BBC World Service Persian Radio

British–Iranian relations

It is clear that Britain and Iran have enjoyed a complex and contested relationship for centuries during which rivalry and admiration, suspicion and friendship have all been present in their bilateral relations.[1] From the nineteenth century, the British started to become interested in Iran since it lay on the land route to India. Slowly, they began to discover other interests, buying rights to conduct banking, print currency, explore for minerals, run transit lines and even grow tobacco. In 1913, the British government achieved a contract under which all Iranian oil became its property and in 1919 it imposed an 'agreement' that gave it control of Iran's army and treasury, prompting anti-British outrage that has long simmered.[2] Britain's occupation of Iran during World War II, when it was a critical source of oil and a transit route for supplies to keep Soviet Russia fighting, was harsh. Famine and disease spread as the British requisitioned food for their troops. Prime Minister Mohammad Mossadeq's push for Iranian oil nationalization in the 1950s meant the British packed their bags, while American 'advisors' became the new external force. And while, after 1979, the revolution and the hostage crisis, America became known as the 'Great Satan', the 'Little Satan' of Britain was often thought to be even more influential in Iranian affairs.

Since the early twentieth century, the formal diplomacy between the two countries has been matched with evolving forms of public diplomacy and what is increasingly in the twenty-first century called 'cultural diplomacy'. From the late 1930s, there was an important role for the cultural attachés working in the embassies in Tehran who organized film screenings and theatrical events that attracted Iranians and promoted a broad notion of their particular national culture. Such activities became more organized and developed through the expansion of the BBC World Service (of which more shortly) and the establishment of the British Council (Anjoman-e Iran o Engelis) in Tehran in 1942. Somewhat later (in the 1950s), but with the same intentions, the US established the United States Information Agency (USIA) and the Iran–America Society (Anjoman-e Iran o Emrika) in Tehran. After 1979, all branches of these institutes, together with those of their German and French counterparts, were shut down.[3] The British Council was only allowed to re-open some 23 years later, to be closed again in 2009.

So it is evident that various kinds of public diplomatic practices were in place long before the term was coined and granted analytic status. It is also clear that from the beginning, while Western analysts and BBC practitioners wished to separate public diplomacy from propaganda, the Iranian authorities, whether royalist or Islamist, have not accepted the distinction.

BBC Persian Service and Reza Shah

The establishment of the BBC Persian Service under Foreign Office direction was driven by the political exigencies of World War II, as we have seen, but also by concerns over Reza Shah Pahlavi's sympathies for Nazi Germany, the fact that many

Iranians were listening to Berlin Radio and the related fact that the British war propaganda was not working very effectively.

Reza Shah had come to power in 1923 with the support of the British government. However, declaring Iran neutral, he declined any cooperation in wartime. The British government was most concerned that he might adopt a pro-Hitler position and potentially block the Allied efforts in the East. Some pro-German papers such as the weekly *Nabard*, or the glossy government-funded magazine, *Iran e Bastan*, had begun publication, writing 'increasingly aggressive and unabashed' articles in defence of Hitler and the Third Reich.[4] Hitler was described as a strong man with firm ideas. Moreover, it was becoming clear that many Iranians were listening to Berlin Radio and that the British war propaganda was not working very effectively. Official Persian newspapers were also voluntarily publishing German news and distributing the newspapers free of charge. The British press attaché wrote a letter to the Foreign Office on 20 September 1939 warning of the dangers of this free propaganda.[5] 'Persian papers are supposed officially to report foreign affairs impartially,' he protested. 'In spite of this impartiality there is a tendency towards a prominent display of news made by Germany. German news is reported in great length and frequently receives pride of place in foreign news,' the letter opined.

In October 1939, the Foreign Office prompted the British Legation in Tehran to test the idea with the Iranian authorities of beginning Persian broadcasts from London but the reply was negative: 'The Iranian Government have now definitely expressed the hope that Persian broadcasts from London, will not be inaugurated.'[6] Four months later in February 1940, the Foreign Office wrote to the head of legation in Iran, Sir Reader Bullard, saying that in the list of wartime priorities the Persian broadcasts were placed 'fairly low'.[7] At about the same time Persian broadcasts to counter the Berlin propaganda were transmitted from India. It is important to note the difference between the anti-Berlin propaganda broadcasts and the broadcasts being considered for the BBC Persian Service. The former 'were not in Persian suitable for

Iran' and they were 'audible only in Kerman and Mashhad not reaching Tehran'.[8] Germans jammed these broadcasts according to a report for the Foreign Office and that is why it was felt that 'Persian broadcasts from London may fill the gap'.[9]

From the spring of 1940 the Foreign Office began seriously to consider Persian broadcasts from London. In June, Sir Reader Bullard wrote to the Foreign Office voicing concern that 'British propaganda in Iran is, compared to German, under various disadvantages'.[10] He argued that historical events meant that Britain's political motives were regarded 'with some suspicion' in Iran, a suspicion that Germany, not having the same historical background, 'escapes'. Second, he said that the Germans were far better at propaganda and had several spies working in Iran. He added that many Iranians confirmed this. And they did. 'Everyone used to listen to radio Berlin every night throughout the war, even when Iran was occupied by Anglo–Soviet forces,' the veteran Freedom Front politician and lawyer, Hedayat Matin-Daftari, recalls.[11] 'One of our neighbors had a radio and we used to take it to the roof, everyone used to sit around, even in winter while wrapped up in winter clothes, to listen to the Persian service of Berlin.' The presenter was called Bahram Shahrokh. 'Everyone was pro-German,' Matin-Daftari says.[12] Bullard also reported this praise for Shahrokh amongst Iranians: 'In the eyes of most Persians our case is much weaker than the Germans and Shahrokh, who flatters the vanity of Persians, especially the army, is far more popular.'[13] Bullard added that the British propaganda was 'sometimes pedantic'.[14]

Stevenson of the Legation suggested that the best way of tackling this shortcoming was through having Persian broadcasts from London. A positive note from Lacey Baggallay at the Eastern Department of the Foreign Office suggested that the idea of setting up the BBC Persian Service had been seriously considered:[15] 'I understand that Persian has now been moved high up on the list of languages waiting attention and the Treasury will begin financial assistance to BBC in this matter.'[16] By the summer of 1940 the Foreign Office was asking the Legation in Tehran to find an Iranian translator and to suggest 'an approximate salary likely to be accepted. Hours of work will be short.'[17]

A number of academics were involved in the planning of the service, while many who worked for the service later became academics. Professor Rushbrook Williams of the Ministry of Information was consulted by the Foreign Office on the best arrangements for starting Persian broadcasts, and in June 1940 the Foreign Office suggested sending a professional journalist to work alongside the Press Attaché in Tehran, a Miss Anne Lambton, who of course went on to become one of Britain's most notable experts on Iran.[18] Lambton, who had started her work in the Legation in 1939, had at this stage become the main writer of reports that were translated and read over the Persian broadcasts. In her first report for Professor Williams, Lambton wrote about the economic hardships amongst the lower classes in Iran, but said she found the young and intellectuals happy with Reza Shah's improvements in the standard of living and with the fact that he had put down the tribal raiders.[19] She also found that most Iranians were concerned about the ongoing war, thinking this would create fertile ground for communist influence. The aim of breaking the German government was viewed as selfish and 'almost wicked' by most Iranians, Lambton says. 'On the whole,' she wrote, 'even if the position in Iran is not very encouraging, there is a slight tendency for public opinion to turn away from Germany towards Britain but it is not very marked.'[20]

Issues of language and translation clearly had to be solved and finding appropriate people was not easy. Finally, in August 1940, D. Stephenson, the director of the BBC Eastern Service, informed the Foreign Office that 'Mr. Gladdening would take charge of the proposed BBC newscasts in Persian,'[21] that a number of Iranian students had already been recruited for translation and that Mr Hamzavi of the Iranian Legation was considered an 'ideal man' to take charge of the actual broadcasts. Thus the initial period of development of the BBC Persian Service shows very close communication between the BBC, the Foreign Office and the Legation in Tehran. It is also interesting to note that the

Ministry of Information 'would be contributing' to Mr Hamzavi's salary, which meant that he would leave the Legation. This document clearly indicates that the British Ministry of Information would be paying the salary of a BBC staff member so that he would be more responsive to their requirements and also a person trained at the British Legation, trusted and familiar with the requirements of the British Foreign Office.[22]

By August 1940 the Foreign Office Eastern Department had drawn up a paper entitled 'BBC Broadcasts in Persian',[23] which set out basic operating procedures for 'the guidance of the BBC in the preparation of material for the projected news broadcasts in the Persian language'. The FO was at pains to note that these guidelines are strictly 'intended for the use of the regular British officials only and they should not be shown or communicated to any Persian-speaking official', and continued:

> It is to be hoped that these new broadcasts will be devoted to the straight news of the world and that, while it is understood that the Ministry of Information will supply news telegrams containing items of more local interest, the broadcasts should as far as possible avoid going into Middle Eastern political questions [...] if some particular event requires clarifying or explanation, the Foreign Office will always be willing to advise on the commentary which the BBC would wish to add.[24]

It suggested that Reza Shah should be treated with due sensitivity and diplomacy in these broadcasts because:

> The Shah is not a popular figure but he is still in complete control and is likely to retain power. While gross flattery of his person or his rule should be avoided, he should be presented as an energetic modern-minded ruler, under whose rule Iran has made great economic and cultural progress. Iran's relations with His Majesty's Government are excellent. Emphasis might on suitable conditions be laid on the long-standing traditional friendship between the two countries...and care should be taken not to suggest that HM Government has any influence whatsoever on Iranian policy.[25]

Thus, while 'straight' news was recommended, the propaganda 'spin' was also quite clearly spelled out, including the appearance of BBC neutrality and a stress on the lack of British involvement in domestic Persian politics, a message of vital importance to get across to Iranian listeners. In his first meeting with the Crown Prince, Mohammad Reza, Bullard had reported to the FO that he found the manner of the prince more engaging than his father, although 'the cynical gloom of the father becomes in the son a pessimistic petulance which he does not attempt to restrain'.[26] Bullard was impressed, however, by the young prince's interest in international affairs and his lack of enthusiasm towards war.[27]

On 21 December 1940 a Foreign Office note on behalf of the British Foreign Secretary informed the Iranian Foreign Minister, Mohammad Ali Moghadam, that broadcasts from London would begin for 15 minutes per day four days a week, namely Sunday, Monday, Tuesday and Saturday: 'The service will begin on Saturday 29 December at 16:30 hours GMT on a wavelength of 3132 meters.'[28]

In the first broadcast on 29 December 1940, Hassan Movaghar-Balyuzi, the new young presenter recruited from Iran, followed the line and introduced the BBC broadcasts as the dawning of a new era: 'The BBC Persian Service is aiding a new relationship between the two nations of Britain and Iran.'[29] Abolqassem Taheri, also just recruited from Tehran, suggested that the British press welcomed the opening of the Persian Service as a step towards better relations with Iran.[30] The short 15-minute news bulletins, broadcast four nights a week over the first few months, maintained this position.

By January 1941 the Foreign Office was discussing the question of how to deal with the BBC. The discussion centred around 'a distinction to be made between information and advice to be given to the News Department and the BBC on "hot news" and directives for propaganda for various countries'.[31] The first was to be done by the Liaison Department, which would advise the BBC on the way the Foreign Office thought the BBC should handle the news. 'For instance,' a memo defining the procedure says, 'the

Foreign Office has to tell the BBC at short notice what it thinks of the speech by Roosevelt or Mussolini or a Russian Government declaration.' 'In all such circumstances,' the memo stresses, 'we send the advice via the teleprinter to the News Department of the BBC Home News and by telephone to the Liaison Department of the BBC.'[32] The planning of 'long-term directives' for propaganda campaigns was different, according to the memo. These 'would go to the BBC as instructions with FO backing'. The memo specified that 'directives of propaganda campaigns by the BBC in various countries are to be drawn up by the relevant committee and representatives of the relevant departments and the Foreign Office should be present in order to convey Foreign Office concurrence'. If there was a short space of time between one directive and the next the BBC could simply ask the Liaison Department. As far as BBC talks and analysis were concerned, the directive specified that the BBC was to be in touch with the same department on any issue that it was not sure about. Thus the BBC did not just have to take directives from the Foreign Office. The Ministry of Information could also convey directives and these could at times be very different to those put across by the Foreign Office. The memo indicates that 'the views of the Information Ministry do not always confirm those of the Foreign Office'.[33]

Clearly the BBC Persian Service had been set up at a very critical conjuncture. The war and the success of Nazi propaganda meant that the British government had to keep a close eye on BBC reports. The memo above reflects the dilemma of having to give directives to the BBC on every detail of political developments and the urgency of some, since it was not just the Persian Service but also several other language services that were broadcasting to countries involved in the ongoing war. A distinction needed to be made between overt and covert propaganda[34] and between enemy countries on the one hand and those countries occupied by enemy forces on the other. Iran perhaps fell in the last category because although it was not occupied by the Axis powers, it was nevertheless regarded as housing many enemy spies and its leader was regarded as pro-Nazi. In a memo to the Foreign Secretary,

Anthony Eden, Sir J. Anderson spelled out the common policy for control of covert propaganda in such countries.[35] He called for regular meetings and consultation on propaganda lines between the various ministries involved, including the Foreign Office, Ministry of Information and the War Office. As far as the BBC was concerned the suggestion was that 'the head of News Department and the new Foreign Office advisor to the BBC should each be given one or more assistants who would sit permanently in the Foreign Office and who would be available to carry out verbal enquiries on any points on which their chiefs require guidance.'[36]

About the same time as these preparations were being made, and only one month after the BBC Persian Service had begun, news came of its popularity in key south-western areas of Iran where the major oilfields were run by the British and the Anglo–Iranian Oil Company (AIOC). Mr Elkington of the AIOC wrote to C.W. Baxter at the Foreign Office saying that the feedback from Abadan, Ahwaz and the oilfields suggested that the BBC has 'reliable news in comparison to Axis broadcasts, which have now deteriorated into transparent propaganda and distortion causing either offence or ridicule.'[37]

However, the rhetoric of mutual friendship, which had characterized the first programmes of the BBC Persian Service, did not last very long. Britain was becoming increasingly impatient with Reza Shah's lack of cooperation over the deportation of some 3,000 Germans believed to be resident in Iran; they were thought to be part of a larger espionage operation designed by the Germans in conjunction with the local Qashqai tribe in Iran to block British war efforts. The British had received intelligence that German spies such as Franz Mayer were working in Iran[38] and had intercepted correspondence from Mayer, stating: 'It has become clear to me what gigantic advantage this ally of ours, Nasser Khan Qashqai, offers.'[39] Mayer's documents revealed that Germany had formed several organizations, parties and military bases in this area. The British Legation in Tehran believed 'Germans were aiming to create in southern Persia an area from which resistance to us [UK] could be arranged.'[40] A letter of denial of German activities in Iran, responding to a *Daily Telegraph* article on the subject, was refused publication by the Foreign Office, which argued that Germany had no right to tell British newspapers what to publish.[41] Concern about Nazi propaganda reached new heights early in 1941. Bullard warned early in February that 'the success of German propaganda in Iran and the failure of British propaganda to make any headway against it has been indicated frequently by the press attaché [Anne Lambton] in her reports'.[42]

Reza Shah refused all the Allied demands, arguing that the Germans were mainly engineers employed in his modernization programme. He failed to realize how serious the British and Soviet governments were about dealing with the Nazi threat. As the conduct of the war became more intense, so too did matters with the BBC. On 7 August 1941, Sir Reader Bullard in Tehran wrote in a 'Most Secret' memo entitled 'Propaganda in Persia':[43]

> The question of propaganda against the Shah would be completely altered in the case of a Russian/British ultimatum, which would be followed by military action in a few days in the case of non-compliance. To forestall the Germans and make the prospect of occupation more palatable we might, simultaneously with the ultimatum, release articles and wireless talks about Persia, referring not only to the good points, but also to the great defects of the present regime, e.g. compulsory acquisition of land at dishonestly low prices and the enormous cost of living. By then it should be too late for the Shah to throw himself to the arms of the Germans, while the army – which is anti-Shah – would be encouraged to turn against him rather than obey him.[44]

On 22 August, Bullard sent yet another memo,[45] 'BBC Broadcasts in Persian', to the Foreign Office, suggesting the following line:

> Tribute could be paid to the Shah as a soldier in the early days but it should be hinted that greediness and tyranny have made him a different man. Forcible acquisition of land, forced labor, general poverty and corruption, acute shortage of water, Shah's own wealth

and ownership of factories [...] his monopoly of all prices [...] his involvement with opium trade [...] his bad treatment of soldiers [...] weakness of the political structure [...] Constitution only in name, a powerless parliament, dictated elections [...] could all be highlighted. Also it could be stressed that England has a democratic Government whereas the Shah, like Hitler, thinks the people are like sheep and are only fit to carry orders blindly.[46]

Three days later, on 25 August 1941, in an operation code named 'Countenance', the British and Soviet forces invaded Iran from the south and the north. After the invasion, the British found it impossible to work with Reza Shah. The Foreign Secretary Anthony Eden explained to the Tehran legation that the government had no wish to 'interfere unnecessarily' in Persian internal affairs, but that it was 'clearly difficult for them to operate fully with an administration that had long ceased to represent the wishes of the people'.[47] Even now a large number of Foreign Office documents have been withheld from the files, yet we know that three propaganda films were made by S.F. Stewart in the India Office and sent to Anne Lambton in Tehran to be released during 1941. They were composed mainly of comedy with a political edge.[48] The BBC Persian Service was tasked with broadcasting more items that revealed Reza Shah's autocratic style of leadership and that encouraged the formation of a republican system of government. Abrahamian writes that:

> His Majesty's Government now agreed that the BBC might begin to give various broadcasts in Persian which had been prepared beforehand, starting with talks on Constitutional Government and increasing in strength and colour until all Reza Shah's mismanagement, greed and cruelty were displayed to the public gaze.[49]

Bullard later wrote that 'on numerous occasions the Allies were unable to get even their most essential military requirements without the application of the strongest diplomatic pressure and once or twice the virtual threat of force. We were obliged to interfere regularly and radically in the local administration [...] There were times when we used to wonder whether in the end we might not have to take over the country and run it ourselves.'[50] The shift in tone of the BBC broadcasts may have helped to produce the desired effect.

Shahrokh Golestan, now a well-known film director, interviewed by the Persian Service for the 65th anniversary of Persian broadcasts, vividly remembered listening to the BBC broadcasts:

> Every evening we used to get together with our neighbors to listen to the BBC Persian broadcasts. We all used to sit in a circle in the garden and the radio – which used to be kept on the second floor – would be turned towards the garden so we could all hear it. We listened every night, not just to the BBC, but also to Radio Berlin to make sure we didn't miss anything.[51]

The news bulletins were in fact written by the War Unit of the BBC, translated into Persian and then broadcast either by the new Iranian recruits or by some Persian-speaking British nationals close to the FO or the Ministry of Information. It was direct war reporting in the propaganda style of the day. The pressure by the government on the BBC World Service broadcasts is reflected in an internal BBC account of wartime reporting:

> From the start, there was tension with the government as to how much freedom should be allowed in wartime to the BBC radio news operations and it took time to establish an effective method of working between the BBC and the new Ministry of Information. BBC staff was seconded to the Ministry – and so-called 'vigilants' from the Ministry were on permanent duty in the newsroom, often alongside representatives of the services.[52]

As well as Movaghar-Balyuzi and Taheri, the first recruits to the BBC Persian Service included Mojtaba Minovi, who had come to Britain on a study tour but had stayed on because of fear of persecution in Reza Shah's regime. Minovi later taught Persian at Oxford, became a distinguished scholar of Persian literature and gained a reputation as a serious Iranian intellectual. Massoud Farzaad and Paul Elwell-Sutton, who had worked for the AIOC, were also recruited to strengthen the broadcasts and ensure accuracy of translation.[53] Abbas Dehghan, another of the first generation of Persian Service reporters, recalls the way the service functioned, with British personnel monitoring the orientation of output carefully: 'We read exactly whatever we were given to read. We were not allowed to make any changes. There were a couple of English people who were monitoring what we broadcast. They spoke Persian and they listened carefully.'[54]

Reza Shah viewed the Persian Service with strong suspicion. An influential politician of the era, Nassrollah Fatemi, recalled that the BBC gave nightly reports of Reza Shah's cruelties, leading Reza Shah himself to tell his acting Foreign Minister, Aamery, that he should listen to the BBC in order to understand British policy on his monarchy and how the British were making decisions about his future.[55] Bullard too wrote that the broadcasts by the BBC shocked Reza Shah and that he tried unsuccessfully to convince the Legation to stop them. However, in the Majlis (parliament), the Iranian deputies 'encouraged by the lead given by the BBC' passed a resolution asking for reforms: 'A deputation of them waited upon the Shah on 16 September [1941] to ask him to abdicate.'[56] However, according to the same report, early that morning Reza Shah had received news that the Soviet forces were advancing from Qazvin near Tehran and had already signed a deed of abdication, drafted by Prime Minister Ali Foroughi in favour of the Crown Prince.[57] Soon after Reza Shah's abdication several members of the parliament began openly denouncing the Shah for accumulating vast fortunes, murdering innocent citizens and abusing his title of commander-in-chief of the army. The BBC broadcasts had clearly played their role. Bullard later wrote in his book that 'the Shah was probably aware of his unpopularity among his own people, and from the tone of the Persian broadcasts by the BBC, now permitted to criticize his actions, he must have realized that he could expect little support from HM Government'.[58]

Asa Briggs noted the importance of these BBC broadcasts to Iran in his definitive *War of Words*, writing that 'the British entry into Iran in August 1941 and the subsequent abdication of the Shah seemed to prove the power of broadcasting – a press correspondent described it as the first instance in history in which a ruler has been hurled from the throne by radio.[59] Briggs quotes directly from the BBC correspondent Richard Dimbleby's dispatch from the area echoing the same point: 'I doubt if the power of broadcasting has ever been shown in such a way as by the success of these [Persian Service] broadcasts.'[60]

Nevertheless, the British did not recognize the consequences of their forced occupation of Iran and the longer-term effect that these broadcasts were to have on their relations with Iran and on the image of the BBC for decades to come. The strong anti-British distrust of the 1930s was now turning into fear and resentment towards an occupying force. Furthermore, the British had to secure their war efforts through direct contact with Iranian politicians and interference in the choice of parliamentary deputies, ministers and the Prime Minister. The Allied war effort also caused severe economic hardship on the population and led to bread and wheat shortages.

The press in Iran turned strongly anti-British. Bullard wrote in March 1943 to Anthony Eden that 'the tone of the press has been deplorable' and that 'we are accused of exploiting Persia in the most callous way.'[61] A weekly illustrated newspaper, *Tehran Mossavar*, dated 23 April 1943, appeared with a cartoon depicting Sir Reader Bullard with a drunken English soldier armed with a rifle, looking with satisfaction on a corpse wounded in the neck. Bullard immediately wrote to the Foreign Office: 'I am asking not only for the suppression of the paper but an immediate and severe punishment of all concerned.'[62] In September 1943, Bullard wrote: 'One gets a strong impression that HMG are increasingly moving into a position in which they get all the blame and none of the credit.'[63] He felt there was 'increasing danger that anti-British feeling may grow to a point at which it will be embarrassing to the British interests.'[64]

By 1944, the British government had concluded that BBC Persian broadcasts were more effective than any other propaganda tool they had used previously. Sir Reader Bullard wrote from Tehran that 'these broadcasts carry more weight than statements made in our local broadcasts in Persian and are listened to by a wider audience. This approach would be more effective than supplying the Persian press with material especially prepared for Persian consumption which by the very nature of its presentation is likely to be treated with suspicion.'[65] One consequence was that in February 1944 the Legation in Tehran was promoted to embassy status and Bullard became Ambassador. By April, he had already planned a wider propaganda campaign, extending the activities of the British Council:

> Cultural propaganda is a field in which we have much leeway to make up in Persia. Persian culture connections have been mainly French [...] Under the late Shah the activity of the British Council was very restricted [...] politically the extension of the British Council should be valuable because they give us contact with the younger generation and an opportunity to influence them in the pro-British direction.[66]

The British Council began work in Iran in 1942, had 19 London-appointed staff and was run by J.G. Hanson. It included specialists in science, education, books, the arts and English language. In addition to the Tehran staff, it had officers and centres in Isfahan, Shiraz, Mashhad, Tabriz and Ahvaz. Its budget was £1.3 million, most of which was provided by the Foreign Office.[67] Its task was to influence politics and culture through persuasion and through the English language.[68]

The BBC World Service and the British Council remain the key players in British public diplomacy in 2013, showing not only the longevity but also the efficacy of the two organizations.

So it was World War II that triggered the establishment of the BBC Persian Service under close Foreign Office direction, one of several methods of influencing politics and society in Iran. However, wartime broadcasting has remained exceptional even in today's broadcasting, and, as we will see in the coming chapters, this did not remain the BBC style for very long. Evidence suggests both that Reza Shah himself was listening and considered the Persian Service to be the voice of the British government and that ordinary people listened, despite the fact that the BBC remained closely associated with British political manipulation in Iran. Lambton wrote that although Britain was not held in high regard by the government, nevertheless the Iranian people thought that Reza Shah was brought to power by Britain and held in power by British support: 'This view is indeed held by many with peculiar obstinacy.'[69] Yet Lambton concluded that 'in view of the fact that British influence and prestige is not high in Iran at the moment, it may be argued that this belief is unreasonable'.[70]

As we mentioned at the start of this chapter, early activity of 'public diplomacy' meant that many European embassies were beginning to offer diets of their national culture. The US also became a particularly active player in Iran from the 1950s, driven strongly by a concern with communist infiltration. The Foreign Service of the United States of America, developed a 'propaganda program [...] to create a positive climate for the United States in a cultural context where the image of the United States was threatened by the prospects of the spread of communism'.[71] The targets of the programme, described as the US Information and Educational (USIE) Exchange Program, were the rural sectors of Iran, and US-generated messages were diffused via visual-oriented media to appeal to these rural sectors. Such media included 'films, film-strips, posters, photo displays and exhibits supplemented by radio, press and educational books and pamphlets'.[72] As Dutta-Bergman has argued, the propaganda activity was launched as an integrated communication campaign, with a plethora of media components serving the key purpose of building the image of the US in the Middle East.[73] The public relations exercise included arrangements made by US public affairs officials with Iranian intellectuals to write pro-US stories such as 'Road to Salvation' and 'Contrast between American and Russian Methods in International Affairs'.[74]

The attempt to influence the national elite via education is also documented through US attempts at placing propaganda materials in strategic positions in libraries. A document sent by the American Embassy in Tehran to the Department of State on 12 January 1951 stated that one of the important tasks facing the Embassy was to build new libraries that would circulate topical American magazines such as *Time, Life, Newsweek* and *Reader's Digest*. The libraries could also display photo exhibits, arranged by the Exhibits section, which occasionally and usually indirectly point to the advantages of the American form of government over the communist state.

So Western powers were competing with each other for influence over Iran's educated elite, each promoting their particular national culture, while the US focus was from early on a concern about the growing influence of communist ideas amongst Iranian intellectuals. The period of oil nationalization would see a further mix of foreign rivalry and collusion, which ultimately sealed Iran's fate.

3

The BBC World Service, the British Government and the Nationalization of Iranian Oil

Iran entered a new era after Reza Shah abdicated in 1941. The atmosphere of fear abated. With the end of World War II came better opportunities for reform and for transition to a more democratic form of government. The young shah, Mohammad Reza Pahlavi, was inexperienced and the parliament, rather than the monarch, became the centre for political decision making. A turbulent political period developed, involving serious battles between new political parties over old ideologies. Ideas of nationalism, liberalism, communism and Islam that had been defunct since the Constitutional Revolution of 1906 were revived in ideological battles in the parliament.

In the next 13 years there were as many as 12 premiers and 31 cabinets. At least 12 political parties were formed, but only six survived to play a recognizable role. Some of the older more outspoken politicians who had been sidelined or deported by Reza Shah, such as Ahmad Qavam and Mohammad Mossadeq, came back, as did the communist leaders who had been imprisoned and tortured. The latter set up contacts across major industrial towns of the south such as Abadan and Ahwaz, but also Isfahan, Mashad, Azerbaijan and Mazandaran provinces and 27 of its younger activists set up the Tudeh Party of Iran. Religious leaders too, such as Ayatollah Abolghasem Kashani, came back to play a powerful role between Islam, the monarchy and liberalism. While the old Anglo–Soviet rivalry persisted, Americans became the new power brokers. A much freer press allowed political debate and discussion. It was also the beginning of the Cold War on the international scene and distrust of the Soviet Union was on the rise.

Iranians were searching for new solutions to their old problems of poverty and inequality. At the same time they were weary of foreign interference and foreign intrigue. The Allies had made good use of Iran during the war, not only extracting huge amounts of its oil, but also building large supply bases from which they launched military operations across the Middle East and North Africa. They used Iran as the main supply route for the Soviet war efforts and ordinary Iranians saw their standard of living fall precipitously, with much food diverted from civilian to military use and trucks and railroads used mainly for military purposes. As the war ended and political life resumed, ordinary Iranians were hoping to make good use of their rich oil resources to rebuild their country.

The British now found themselves at the centre of political controversy regarding the control of Iran's oil through the Anglo–Iranian Oil Company (AIOC). The charismatic politician, Mohammad Mossadeq, the leader of the National Front, who was elected to the Fourteenth Majlis in February 1944, used his first speech to attack the British and Reza Shah at the same time.[1] He denounced the British for being at the root of most of the economic problems in Iran because of their hold on oil reserves. More than half of AIOC's profits went directly to the British government, which owned 51 per cent of the shares. Foreign Secretary Ernest Bevin was not exaggerating when he observed that without oil from Iran, there would be 'no hope for our being able to achieve the standard of living at which we are aiming in Great Britain'.[2] As the American journalist Stephen Kinzer observed: 'Iranians found it difficult to generate much sympathy for the British.'[3]

The postwar period was dominated by the question of Iranian oil and overwhelming Iranian public support for nationalization – fiercely contested by the British. The crisis that ensued between Iran and Britain was perhaps a turning point in Iran's history. It brought powerful nations of the world into head-on collision with the nationalist government of Dr Mohammad Mossadeq and led to the Anglo–American coup of August 1953, regarded in retrospect by both powers as a mistake.

Throughout the late 1940s and early 1950s the British government had problems persuading consecutive Iranian governments to continue with its exceptional concessions on oil extraction with the AIOC. The British pointed to Article 21 of the 1933 Agreement signed with the AIOC, which stated that the concession could not be altered or annulled by the Persian government. Undeterred, members of the Majlis demanded that the oil company offer them a better deal and submitted a bill to revoke AIOC's concession. The British offered a Supplemental Agreement to change some of the details without revoking the original principles of the agreement or losing their part ownership. The Iranian parliament fought back. This was a serious dilemma for the British government and, as in Reza Shah's era, they invited the BBC to support them at a difficult moment.

After the war, the British government had decided on new, more indirect ways of influencing politics. The broadcasts of the BBC Persian Service and the work by British Council officials in Iran aimed to influence politics and culture through persuasion. Reader Bullard suggested that: 'When action is taken by a Persian official as a result of persuasion or pressure by a consular officer, the British delegations should, as far as possible, be kept directly in the background and subordinate officials and the public should be allowed and even encouraged to believe that the Persian official acted on his own responsibility and initiative.'[4]

After establishing itself as the leading global broadcaster during the war, the BBC Overseas Service, including the BBC Persian Service, had been incorporated into the BBC's Charter when it came up for renewal in 1946.[5] The Charter guaranteed editorial independence, the BBC being required only 'to receive advice from the Government on our [British] policies towards the countries to which they broadcast in the national interest'.[6] From the start, there was a general attempt to safeguard the editorial independence of the BBC from government, since this was seen by the broadcaster as the cornerstone of the credibility of its international broadcasts and therefore of its impact. The BBC World Service and languages services were all included in this new package for creating trust and credibility around the world. The 1946 Broadcasting White Paper proposed by the Labour government set out the relationship between government and the BBC, which still pertains today. It reads:

> The Government intends that the Corporation should remain independent in the preparation of programmes for overseas audiences, although it should obtain from the government departments concerned such information about conditions in those countries and the policy of His Majesty's government towards them as will permit it to plan its programmes in the national interest.[7]

Nevertheless, in the documents of the Foreign Office there are several examples in the era under analysis clearly indicating that the government considered the BBC Persian Service a useful tool for making relevant announcements and carrying political lines. When, for example, on 6 November 1948, a meeting took place in London between the British and Iranian foreign ministers discussing Iran's constitution, the Foreign Office asked the embassy in Tehran: 'Do you wish BBC to say that no discussion on the constitution took place?'[8] And in a secret telegram later the same day: 'BBC are instructed to issue withdrawal of their news item.'[9] The next day BBC news of the meeting was adjusted to carry the instruction as follows:

The Persian Foreign Minister who has been on a private visit to Britain has now returned to Paris. While he was in London he took the opportunity of renewing his acquaintance with Mr. Bevin. Earlier reports that the two ministers discussed Persian's internal affairs are quite untrue.[10]

On 4 February 1949 an incident heightened the Anglo–American fear of Soviet intrusion in Iran and provided the Shah with an excuse for suppression. An unsuccessful attempt was made on the Shah's life as he arrived at Tehran University to attend a ceremony. The assailant, Fakhr Arai, was later described by the Information Minister as a member of the Tudeh Party and used to tighten the grip on the Soviet-backed Tudeh Party. Moreover, to quell unrest, in November 1949, Ayatollah Kashani was exiled[11] and Dr Mossadeq was asked to retire to his country estate.[12] These outcomes benefited the British since the power centre seemed to be shifting from the parliament to the Shah. They preferred to deal with the young Shah rather than the barrage of criticism in the Majlis.

Following two failed attempts at forming a new, more cooperative government, the Shah was encouraged by the British to bring in General Ali Razmara in June 1950 hoping he would have the military power to curb 'the frustration, wide-spread distress and increasing popular unrest during the winter'.[13] Razmara had good relations with Britain and the US.[14] He told the British that he could win approval of their Supplemental Agreement if they revised it but, much to his dismay, the British rejected the proposal out of hand. Meanwhile, the AIOC tried to convince General Razmara to re-open negotiations on a 50/50 profit-sharing basis and to make this known to the general public. Razmara did not accept because he knew the parliament would reject it out of hand.

In April 1950, Britain sent a new ambassador to Iran, Sir Francis Shepherd, who had been stationed in authoritarian states such as Peru, El Salvador and Belgian Congo. About the same time, the completion of the results of parliamentary elections to the Sixteenth Majlis showed that six members elected from the capital, Tehran, were from the National Front. Moreover, both the renowned anti-British politicians Mossadeq and Kashani had been elected.[15]

> Kashani was fiercely anti-Western, hated liberal ideas and believed that Muslims should obey secular laws only if they were in harmony with Islamic legal traditions. His father had been killed fighting the British in Mesopotamia during World War I and he was held in a British prison camp during World War II suspected of being a Fifth Columnist. Once elections were announced he ran from his exile in Beirut to take part and won a seat.[16]

Shepherd noted to the Foreign Secretary, Ernest Bevin, that: 'The National Front appears to have no programme other than opposing the Government of the day and the Supplementary Oil Agreement.'[17] Kinzer describes the moment vividly: 'With the bearded holy man Kashani and the Swiss educated aristocratic Mossadeq stoking the anti-British fire, opinion in the Majlis turned ever more strongly against the Supplemental Agreement.'[18] The British Foreign Office was furious. In its annual report on Iran's internal situation it criticized the action of these deputies as being driven by 'their own personal interests.'[19] Deputies had been 'bullied by a small but vocal minority into refusing a remunerative oil agreement at a time when the national finances were low', the report said. Thus the tide was turning against British interests. Moreover, the Soviet-backed semi-clandestine Tudeh Party was supporting nationalization and pushing for improved conditions for the working class in Iran as a whole, with a special focus on the oil workers in the southern oilfields of Khuzestan.

In the summer of 1950, the Americans sent in a new ambassador, Henry Grady. They suggested to the British that the AIOC should modify the terms of the Supplemental Agreement 'to make it more palatable to the Persians.'[20] On 20 June 1950 the Majlis set up the Mixed Oil Commission, 'dominated by the National Front which was unfavorable to the British proposal for a Supplemental Agreement.'[21] Mossadeq became the chairman of the Commission that met twice a week to discuss the terms of the Supplemental Agreement. However, the terms were rejected and the Supplemental Agreement was withdrawn from parliament on 26 December 1950.

On 19 February 1951, Mossadeq put in a proposal to the Commission for the nationalization of oil. A lead article in the National Front newspaper, *Keshvar*, encapsulates the general anti-British mood in Iran. It directly addressed the British Prime Minister just before the vote on the nationalization of oil:

> How can Mr. Attlee have the right of nationalizing British heavy industries and we cannot have the right to nationalize our oil industry? Mr. Furlong [the British Foreign Office representative visiting Iran at the time] must tell the high authorities including Mr. Eden that Persians are no longer prepared to come to any compromise with the AIOC. In fact the Persian people now detest the company. Persians are no longer prepared to come to any compromise with that company.[22]

In such a stalemate, the persuasive force of the BBC was brought in to help. On 1 March 1951, the British Ambassador suggested to the Foreign Office that it would be useful 'to inspire the BBC's Persian Service at this present stage in the oil question to write a talk bringing out the points we feel can usefully be made in this context':[23]

> They [the points] should be cast in such a way that nationalization is not and cannot be, a purely internal Persian problem. They are also designed to show the impracticality of nationalization and the financial and other losses, which any such move may involve.[24]

The memorandum suggested publicity directives for the BBC with seven possible lines of argument.[25] At the core of the publicity was the idea that the nationalization of oil would be detrimental to Iran's future economic progress and might give rise to financial losses. The BBC talk was also to argue that nationalization would harm Iran's reputation internationally and have adverse effects on the industry as a whole. It was specified that since 'the voting on oil nationalization takes place on 5th March, the broadcast should go out on the day before'.[26] Three days later, and just a day before the vote in the Majlis, all these points were articulated in a BBC Persian Service broadcast written by an unnamed diplomatic correspondent.[27] The talk argued that:

> In the first place it must be remembered that the Anglo–Iranian oil company has invested vast sums of money [...] the arbitrary cancellation of the oil agreement and the failure to honor an international agreement would seriously damage Persian credit and reputation in the world [...] it would be difficult to see how Persia thinks of paying a huge sum to which an international tribunal would certainly consider the company entitled [...] and there is the company's expenditure of tens of millions of pounds.[28]

In the spring of 1951, the BBC was receiving letters from Persian listeners at the rate of 25 per day, according to the BBC handbook for the year 1952: 'These correspondents, widespread throughout the country, asked innumerable questions concerning British life, thought and policy.'[29] When the oil crisis arose, these correspondents provided 'an excellent opportunity for putting forward the British point of view in the form of replies to questions raised by the Persians', said the handbook, and answers were provided in the programmes dedicated to listeners' letters.

The National Front continued its vigorous campaign for oil nationalization and Prime Minister Razmara was called on by the Oil Commission to state whether nationalization was practicable or not. However, on 7 March 1951 a member of Fedayeen-e Islam (Devotees of Islam), a group suspected of being closely associated with Kashani, assassinated Razmara. The *New York Times* referred to Razmara as 'a brilliant professional soldier who had acquired commanding status as a result of the defeat of the communist puppet regime in Azerbaijan [in 1945]'. He was seen as 'best able to keep the divergent political elements together' and his murder, concluded the *New York Times*, 'can only play into the hands of the Communists'.[30]

At this stage the Americans were not wholeheartedly supporting the British position on oil. Details of exchanges and meetings between officials seen in the British Foreign Office and American State Department documents reveal the frustration of the British in obtaining the approval of their US allies. The British Embassy in Washington was the scene of several such meetings and at one such session, on 11 April, the British found 'the Americans will not budge from their present assessment of the strength of Persian attachment to nationalization nor their conviction that the UK is running grave risks in continuing to under-estimate it'.[31] A report on the meeting concluded that the Americans 'will be unable to secure their positive support [for the British] for the next move on Persia without making a bow at nationalization'.[32] The Americans had also expressed concern on several occasions that the British 'should not use force of any sort, including a naval demonstration' near the AIOC refinery in Abadan, 'which permits the Russians to move force into Persia'.[33]

On 15 March the Mixed Oil Commission presented a resolution to the Parliament for nationalization of oil, which was adopted and, five days later, also approved by the Senate. A nine-point bill providing for oil nationalization was quickly drawn up and it received royal assent on 1 May. The Shah had little choice in the matter, given the general public's support for oil nationalization as clearly reflected in the press.

When the BBC interviewed Ahmad Maleki, an active member of the National Front and the editor of *Setareh* news-paper, it adopted the same points as provided by the Foreign Office.[34] The first BBC question refers to Iran's action as being 'unilateral', to which Maleki responds: 'This is the right of a nation to nationalize its oil resources.' The second question refers to Iran as 'breaking the terms of an agreement', to which Maleki angrily responds: 'This was voted by the parliament.' The third question asks: 'Don't you think this damages Iran's international reputation?' Maleki says he thinks completely the opposite since Iran's independence would benefit her international standing.[35] The text of the interview was sent on 22 May 1951 to the BBC Persian Service for broadcast in Persian.

Meanwhile, in May 1951, Dr Mossadeq was voted Prime Minister. In his opening speech Mossadeq moved immediately to the issue of oil, linking it to Iran's independence from the UK.[36] He thanked the deputies for approving oil nationalization: 'you have proved that an Iranian never allows her home to be taken over by foreigners'.[37] In June, Mossadeq sent a committee of five to the southern Khuzestan province to begin the process of taking over the oil installations from the AIOC. He also announced martial law and sent the army down, fearing a possible attack by the British. On 23 June, Mossadeq announced officially that the operations for the takeover of the installations had been completed and the National Iranian Oil Company (NIOC) was now in place. The temporary board of the NIOC gave the AIOC staff one week to decide whether they wanted to remain in the employment of the new organization or not. The staff, which was mainly British, gave a unanimous negative answer.

On 26 June 1951 all shipments of oil from Abadan were suspended.[38] The British government tried to forestall further action by Mossadeq by asking the International Court of Justice in The Hague for an interim injunction that called upon the Persian government not to prejudice the position of the AIOC. The Foreign Office informed the BBC that the situation was becoming dangerous and that Britain might have to send in parachute troops.[39] In such a case the BBC would have to be brought in to help in making the necessary announcements for the rescue of AIOC British staff, under the operation known as Midget. According to a top-secret memo, at their meeting on Monday 18 June the Chiefs of Staff considered a telegram from the Commander-in-Chief, Middle East, on the subject of 'BBC announcements in connection with Midget' and the request was forwarded to 'the BBC Persian Programme'.[40] They further considered that the draft of the announcement should be kept ready in conjunction with 'the dropping of leaflets at the time of the operation Midget'. Moreover, 'an afternoon broadcast at

13:30' and a 'morning service at 7:30' were added to the Persian broadcasts in addition to the usual 20:30 transmission.[41] The afternoon broadcast was dropped after 27 August 1951 when Britain gave up its plans for the military invasion of Iran. That slot has since been kept for wartime broadcasting in the Persian Service. It has been used whenever there has been regional danger of war; for example, during the Persian Gulf War and during and after the invasion of Afghanistan in 2001.[42]

On 5 July the International Court of Justice, in response to a request from the British government, suggested certain provisional measures and ordered that the two governments should not do anything to pre-judge the case. The Iranian government rejected this, suggesting it was interference in the internal affairs of Iran. Mossadeq was, however, more responsive to an offer of mediation by the US president Harry Truman, who wrote to him describing the crisis as 'so full of dangers to the welfare of your own country [Iran] and Great Britain and of all the free world'.[43] Truman recommended adherence to the recommendations of the International Court and asked if he could send his closest advisor, Averell Harriman, to Iran. Mossadeq wrote back: 'In the light of our knowledge of Mr. Harriman's personality and his vast experience and considering the fact that he will act as your representative, the Iranian government welcomes this gesture.' However, Mossadeq included an important condition in his letter: 'provided of course that our indisputable national rights are respected in accordance with the laws concerning the nationalization of the oil industry'.[44] Harriman arrived in Tehran on 16 July but swiftly reported to Truman his lack of success. The British delegation led by Lord Privy Seal Stokes, which had arrived on 3 August for talks with Iran, also did not achieve an agreement. Harriman's report to Truman on 15 September 1951 showed his disapproval of the method adopted by Mossadeq: 'The seizure by any government of foreign-owned assets,' said the report, 'without either prompt, adequate and effective compensation or alternative arrangements satisfactory to the former owners is, regardless of the intent, confiscation rather than nationalization.'[45]

A telegram of 'particular secrecy' from the British Embassy in Tehran stressed that there was no 'disagreement between the US embassy and ourselves that what Persia needs is a strong, constructive, competent and honest government, whereas in fact the present one is a weak, negative and corrupt one'.[46] It predicted that there was 'a danger that the longer Mossadeq remains in power, the greater the danger of a communist regime becomes'. Yet the American position at this stage was that it was vital that Iran should receive economic assistance, since 'unless Mossadeq received financial help from the West, he would obtain it immediately from the Soviet bloc'.[47]

However, the British thought it would be very difficult for the Soviets to take advantage of the situation or give any effective help to Iran.[48] They believed Mossadeq mostly wanted to 'indulge in playing off one great power against another'.[49] The 1951 annual report from the British Embassy in Tehran concluded that while 'relations with His Majesty's Government deteriorated steadily, other nations gained popularity according to their attitude to the oil dispute and the fight against imperialism'.[50]

The issue of oil nationalization had become intertwined with potential Soviet invasion. In a memorandum on 10 October 1951 the US Joint Chiefs of Staff described the dangers if 'Iran passes to the domination of the USSR', and predicted 'an expansion of the Soviet Empire to the Persian Gulf and the Indian Ocean' and 'communist domination' in the region. They feared 'the USSR would be permitted to develop facilities for the delivery of Iranian oil to the territory of the USSR'. The memorandum recommended that Iran's orientation towards the US was more important than 'the desirability of supporting British oil interests in Iran'.[51]

The US fear of Soviet domination could only have been aggravated when the British submitted their case to the UN Security Council and the Soviet representative backed Iran's right to her oil resources. Mossadeq spoke passionately in defence of Iran's rights and the fact that the British had 'taken away the wealth of Iran in the past 25 years and now Iranians want to reserve their right to their natural resources'.[52] The Soviet Ambassador to the UN thus vetoed the British proposal against Iran.

The report of the British Embassy in Tehran described 1951 as the worst year in Anglo–Iranian relations, saying: 'The fault can be placed at the door of one man – Dr. Mossadeq.'[53] It described Iran's Prime Minister as 'an honest but misguided and often purblind patriot', whose 'distinct demagogy, his single minded obstinacy and his total lack of constructive ideas' had rendered an agreement impossible: 'Dr. Mossadeq has fanned national pride into intolerance, religious revival into fanaticism and a desire for independence into stubborn isolationism and xenophobia.'[54]

This rapidly became the British line on Mossadeq. *The Times* newspaper said 'the fundamental causes which have brought this conflict to a head are the stupidity, greed and the lack of judgment of the ruling classes in Iran'.[55] *The British Point of View* was the name of a document[56] handed to all reporters. It explained why the British government took the dispute with the Persian government to the UN Security Council. It highlighted those parts of the AIOC agreement with Iran that specified that the Iranian government had 'bound itself not to nationalize the oil enterprise of the company'. It complained about 'increasing interference of the Persian authorities in the company's operations' to explain why it had applied for an injunction. It then explained how Iran had ignored the injunction as 'they interfered more and more with their operations and finally expelled the [British] technicians from Abadan'. The text also claimed Iran had 'consistently denied the competence of the international court. Indeed Mr. Mossadeq has made it quite clear that if the court decides the dispute comes within its jurisdiction, he will continue to refuse to abide by any ruling which it makes.'[57] The Americans too began putting the blame on Mossadeq who had in their view 'used and abused American good-will, encouraging the US to play the "honest broker" in the oil dispute in order to put the blame for its failure on "the shoulders of Ambassador Grady and Mr. Harriman"'.[58]

The sudden surge of adverse reporting on Mossadeq had its effect on the BBC Persian Service broadcasters. Many of the staff of the BBC Persian Service felt an affinity not with the UK or their employers in the BBC, but with oil nationalization and with Mossadeq. Some personnel simply slipped away. Anvaar, a Persian broadcaster, recalls that when 'it came to reporting adversely on Mossadeq, suddenly for two weeks all Iranian broadcasters disappeared. The BBC had no choice but to bring in English people who spoke Persian, because the Iranians had gone on strike. The broadcasts were all in a Persian with a strong English accent.'[59] Another veteran broadcaster, Abbas Dehghan, noted that broadcasts were mainly translations of British analysis, and even the satire and cultural programmes were written by the British and translated by the Persian broadcasters.[60] The situation was different, according to Dehghan, when it came to Mossadeq: 'no Iranian was prepared to say anything against Mossadeq. Nobody would be disrespectful of Mossadeq.' Another veteran Persian Service broadcaster, Abolqassem Taheri, went a step further, claiming 'with two or three of my colleagues I declare openly that we shall follow our government's [Mossadeq's] attitude whatever it may be.'[61]

At such a crisis point, it was difficult for the Persian Service to maintain both the trust of the listeners and those who employed them at the BBC. Yet Norman Kemp, who called himself 'a regular Abadan reporter', wrote in his book *Abadan* (1953) about the importance of BBC broadcasts during the crisis period:

> The Persian authorities had suspended the Company's [AIOC] daily newspaper and each afternoon and evening the oilmen huddled around radio sets to listen to BBC overseas broadcasts for up-to-date information. If Abadan or Teheran were not mentioned in the bulletins the staff was despondent, believing the omission was an augury of defeat.[62]

Kemp's account of this crisis period shows how tension between the UK and Iran was seeping down to both Iranian and international journalists who had come to Abadan to report. Kemp's

account also illustrates how the AIOC and the British government dominated the international news reporting of the crisis.[63]

Tehran Radio, controlled by Mossadeq's government, was
also used for comments and propaganda against the British
government and the BBC Persian Service. Thus the pro-
nationalization majority did not always trust the Service's broadcasts. Hussein Makki, the right-hand man of Mossadeq, attacked
British conduct and singled out the BBC for blame when in
August 1951 he accompanied the US president's representative
Harriman to Abadan to see the squalid conditions of the living
quarters of the Persian oil workers:

> Should the Mossadeq Government suffer defeat, Soviet prop-
> aganda will convince the people that only with Russian aid can
> the Iranians succeed. It is in this that the greatest danger lays. The
> desire of the British capitalist is that nationalization should fail.
> They are shareholders in the AIOC and they are trying in every
> possible way and through underhand methods to bring down the
> Mossadeq Government. This is being done with the aid of the
> Persian-language broadcasts and the commentaries of the BBC,
> by inspired and biased articles in the British press.[64]

By the end of January 1952, on the request of Mossadeq, most
British consulates were closed in Iran; 22 British employers of
the consulates were called in and told to 'pack their bags and
get ready to go back to the UK'.[65] The British government had
'strongly contested the decision and put its members on high
alert'.[66] Four days later the paper reported that the British ambassador, Sir Francis Shepherd, had been called back to London,
although the official British line was that 'the decision was unre-
lated to the closure of the consulates'. At this stage both countries
only had *chargé d'affaires* in each other's capital and it appeared
that diplomatic relations had been severely damaged.[67] 'Mossadeq
told the British you punched us, now take our punch,' reads the
front-page headline of *Bakhtar Emruz* (the main newspaper) on
22 January. Six days later the headline became more confident in
tone: 'British Eastern policy doomed to failure.'[68] 'We must show

the world that we are capable of looking after our own natural resources,' said Mossadeq in a radio broadcast for the Persian New Year. 'We must also show the world that we wish to do this in a free and independent way.'[69] By April, Mossadeq produced documents of British interference in Iran.[70] He said in an interview with *Etelaat* newspaper on 13 April:

> Since the British government in such cold blood denies having interfered in the affairs of Iran except in order to preserve our independence, the Government has no choice but to publish these documents as living proof of this illegitimate British interference in Iran's affairs for several centuries.[71]

At a meeting between the British and US officials in the Foreign Office in London in February 1952, they agreed that over the two months that had passed 'Mossadeq's position had strengthened.'[72] Yet they offered no remedy to combat communism, although it was decided that it would be unwise to offer Mossadeq any financial assistance despite the fact that the 'economic situation was serious'. They discussed possible scenarios including the staging of a coup against Mossadeq, and whether the Shah commanded enough loyalty: 'and what are the chances of the army being able to stage a successful coup if called on by the Shah?'[73]

On 9 June 1952 the International Court at The Hague heard an impassioned speech by Dr Mossadeq in defence of Iran's right to nationalize oil. The judgment of the court was in favour of Iran. It was decided, however, that the case of AIOC should be seen as distinct from the British government. In other words the British government had never been party to an agreement with Iran and these governments had no claim over each other. The AIOC called for an international boycott of Iranian oil. According to Kinzer[74] the British began to make it impossible for the NIOC to function and the first tactic they used was the discreet sabotage of the oil refinery. There were also no technicians to run the refinery and when the Iranian government placed advertisements to recruit international experts British diplomats would ensure no one made it to Abadan. Kinzer writes that 'they persuaded

Sweden, Austria, France and Switzerland to deny exit visas to interested applicants.[75] This well-coordinated campaign made it impossible for Iran to produce oil.

The change in British government also proved decisive. Attlee had done whatever was possible on behalf of the AIOC, but since October 1951, when Winston Churchill came to power, he had tried hard to gain American support and thereby give the oil dispute a more international appearance. Moreover, at the American Embassy in Tehran, Loy Henderson had replaced the US ambassador Henry Grady, who had always pressed for negotiations and supported Mossadeq. 'The end of the year,' said the annual report of the Foreign Office, 'saw Persia with her great oil industry stopped, her finances in perilous condition, her economy gradually running down, the authority of the government impaired and an already inefficient machinery of administration at a virtual standstill.'[76] The social and economic crisis in Iran intensified.

The British encouraged the Shah to dismiss Mossadeq and replace him with Ahmad Qavam.[77] But the plan did not work. Mossadeq had won a clear majority and the National Front held all Tehran seats in the Seventeenth Majlis. Much encouraged by this success, when Mossadeq presented the list of ministers to the Shah for approval, he kept the defence portfolio for himself. The Shah, as the Commander-in-Chief, used his constitutional right to reject this and Mossadeq resigned on 5 July 1952. The Shah used the opportunity to replace him with Qavam. But these moves were met by an uproar in Parliament and a call for a national strike. Qavam fell and Mossadeq came back even more powerful.

In a conversation with the British chargé, George Middleton, Mossadeq had complained about 'AIOC agents that were working everywhere'.[78] He also wrote a letter to the Embassy reporting about 'anonymous letters from the Iranian embassy in London', alleging that there was 'a covert action underway' to assassinate him and 'the operation is directed by a certain Major Healy'.[79] As part of their efforts to paralyse Iran's economy, Britain blocked the sale of Iranian oil, and instructed the Bank of England to make it practically impossible for Iran to convert her sterling balances. To make sure Iran remained short of foreign funds, Britain consistently stopped the US from giving Iran any financial assistance.[80]

Henderson tried to design a formula by which Iran could sell oil to the US on a long-term basis through an international company:[81] 'An international oil corporation will be created to ship and market Persian oil and the question of compensation to AIOC will be referred to an international body for settlement.'[82] Mossadeq rejected the plan,[83] saying Iran had never refused to sell oil on the international market, whether to AIOC or any other organization, and therefore the creation of an international organization in which the Americans were to participate had no benefits for Iran and would not take the oil crisis any further.[84] Mossadeq also rejected repeated attempts by the US to renew Iran's Mutual Defence Agreement, saying that this would undermine Iran's independence.[85]

The British reported that Ambassador Henderson, who had 'evidently staked a lot on the negotiations, confessed himself discouraged'.[86] They saw this as a chance to begin influencing the Americans to favour their plans to confront Mossadeq. The US Central Intelligence Agency wrote:

> Mossadeq shows little shame, conscience or dignity [...] In order to avoid weakening his internal position he refuses to give the US a clear assurance that US aid would be used to strengthen Iran's military ability to defend herself.[87]

During January 1953, Mossadeq had in fact written two messages to US authorities requesting economic rather than military aid, but President Dwight Eisenhower, who had just come to power, made this conditional on both the resolution of the oil problem and more importantly on Iran's acceptance of the renewal of the military aid package. Eisenhower, as a military man, had one main concern and that was relations between Mossadeq and the Soviet Union. There was also serious concern about the Tudeh Party's increasing strength in the army. Henderson wrote in April 1953 that 1,600 Tudeh members were working inside the army and that if this continued over the next five years the party would have a strong presence in the Iranian army.[88] He felt Iran must agree the American military package to survive any possible Soviet attack. The British played on that American sensitivity, warning about the Perso–Soviet frontier protocol signed by Mossadeq and the improvements in relations between the two countries.[89]

Although Iran was enduring major economic difficulties, Mossadeq made an impassioned speech in Parliament saying he would not compromise Iran's sovereignty for the sake of oil revenues. He argued that Iran's independence was worth far more than any oil revenue and challenged the British by proposing an economic austerity programme based on an oil-less economy.

With increasing economic pressure many of the former allies of Mossadeq began to disagree with his harsh measures, even including his closest National Front colleagues. On 4 January 1953 he made another speech reminding his supporters that: 'The British did not rule us by brute force or military force but by intrigue and by creating dissent and disunity amongst us.'[90] He pleaded with the public that he had done all in his power to create reform and to ensure that the independence of Iran remained intact, but that the 'intrigues of the British and innumerable difficulties created by her in the way of resolving the oil situation had delayed reforms'. These reforms were needed to 'induce the enemy [Britain] to abandon its efforts to prevent the solution of the oil problem'.[91]

The British Embassy in Tehran, concerned about the possible outcome of these developments, drew an appropriate 'line for News Department and the BBC'.[92] Its points, written out in full detail, were given to the BBC following a briefing at the Foreign Office on 19 March 1953. The line ordered minimum comment by officials about the situation in Iran and about Mossadeq. It stressed that Mossadeq had rejected all 'fair and equitable' solutions and all Anglo–US proposals for the settlement of the oil. Officials were also to stress that Mossadeq had offered inaccurate information on compensation figures and revenues and on the claim that Britain had burdened the Iranian economy through its action. They were asked not to comment on counter proposals and to avoid issuing the text of the Compensation Agreement.

Laurence Paul Elwell-Sutton, the British scholar and one of the first staff of the BBC Persian Service, who had later worked in the AIOC, wrote in passionate defence of Iranian oil nationalization. In his book *Persian Oil* (1955), he mentions the role of BBC broadcasts in persuading Iranians not to support oil nationalization:

> From London where the BBC had doubled and trebled its transmissions in the Persian language, Persians were told that the British staff [of AIOC] would leave if the company was not given its way. And if this happened the oil industry would collapse. And if the oil industry collapsed, listeners were warned, Persia's economic system would collapse too.[93]

Elwell-Sutton adds that Tehran radio also reported propaganda material attacking the British Ambassador and the British government on a regular basis. Yet he was sympathetic to the strike action taken by the Iranian staff of the BBC Persian Service during the oil crisis. 'This radio propaganda was offensive,' he wrote, 'no wonder the BBC's Persian announcers on several occasions patriotically refused to speak the lines handed to them. British propaganda services, on instructions from the Eastern Department of the Foreign Office, attempted to whitewash Britain's record in Persia by plugging the work of British scholars in the Persian language.'[94] This might not be the earliest example, but it is a significant one of how the innovative World Service practice of employing nationals to speak (only later to actually write) the news produced profound conflicts of interest for the employees. As mentioned, for many Iranians, the solution was to remove themselves.

By March 1953 *The Times* of London reported that opposition to Mossadeq had escalated and 'all the political parties that wish to overthrow him have cooperated in the last two days in waging the most serious anti-government campaign that Dr. Mossadeq has faced since he became Prime Minister two years ago'.[95] They accused him of causing tension by his provocative broadcasts from Radio Tehran. Mossadeq, on the other hand, blamed 'foreign agents' for the disorder and called for a referendum to dissolve the parliament;[96] 2 million voted in his favour with only 1,000 against.[97]

On 15 August the Imperial Guards arrested many of Mossadeq's ministers and presented him with a decree signed by the Shah dismissing him and appointing General Fazlollah Zahedi as Prime Minister. Mossadeq in turn arrested the officers who had presented him with the decree and disregarded it. The Shah, who had gone to the Caspian on 13 August to avoid suspicion, was fully aware of the coup plot, but had conveyed to the US and the British that he wanted it done in such a way that it had the appearance of a formal constitutional decision with the relevant letters for replacing the Prime Minister.[98] From the Caspian he had sent coded messages to his trusted friends to deliver the letters. So when he heard that the plan had not worked at the initial stage he was dismayed. He assumed that he had been 'betrayed or that the code had been broken'.[99] The US advised the Shah that he should leave the country and explain in a statement that this was because 'his authority was no longer respected and because he desired to avoid bloodshed'.[100] The advice stressed that he should say in the statement that 'far from having attempted to organize a coup he was himself the victim of a coup d'etat carried out by Mossadeq'.[101]

An account of a conversation between the US Ambassador in Tehran and the Shah on 30 May 1953 reveals that General Zahedi had been selected by both the Americans and the British to become the next Prime Minister at least three months prior to the coup.[102] Although the Shah did not approve of Zahedi, saying 'he was not an intellectual giant', he was encouraged to do so with the promise of aid from the US government.[103]

An important Foreign Office document, only released to the public in 2008, shows the initial stages of planning of the coup by the US and the UK to have been already developed in April 1953 after the failure of the oil negotiations.[104] A top-secret memo from the British Embassy in Washington to the Foreign Office says that 'an attempt may be made to displace Mossadeq, preferably but not necessarily by constitutional means'.[105] It specifies that the leader of the movement will be Zahedi, who ironically is believed to have 'the support of the majority in Majlis'. The memo then specifies that this could either be by means of 'a vote of non-confidence in the Majlis or by coup d'etat'. It asserts that the US has not fully worked out the idea yet and believes 'there should be no hurry to comment publicly on an attempt to oust Mossadeq in its initial stages'. According to the memo: 'the American position was that any regime which supported the Shah and opposed communism would be better than Mossadeq's – with the exception of one headed by Kashani'. The document clearly reflects the fact that the new US administration was thinking far more in line with the British government. The document makes it clear at every stage, as far as publicity about the matter was concerned, that the US government wanted to have the approval of the British government as to when and how to present the case to the public.

In June 1953 the plan of a coup proposed by the British and worked over by the Americans was discussed in Washington in a meeting chaired by the Secretary of State John Foster Dulles, with a team that included his brother, the CIA chief Allen Dulles, and the CIA operative, Kermit Roosevelt.[106] The latter was tasked with implementing a coup to remove the democratically elected Prime Minister Mossadeq and to replace him with Zahedi. The coup was finally implemented on 19 August 1953.[107] Many years later, on 17 March 2000, the former US Secretary of State, Madeleine Albright, admitted to the role played by the US in these words:

> In 1953 the United States played a significant role in orchestrating the overthrow of Iran's popular Prime Minister, Mohammed Massadegh. The Eisenhower Administration believed its actions were justified for strategic reasons; but the coup was clearly a

setback for Iran's political development. And it is easy to see now why many Iranians continue to resent this intervention by America in their internal affairs.[108]

Roosevelt provided a detailed account of the operation, code-named Ajax, in his book *Counter Coup*.[109] When the book was in the process of publication in 1977 the Shah's chief of protocol, Assadollah Alam, told him about it and described the book as 'undesirable'.[110] In 1977, when the Shah was facing the beginnings of a revolution to topple him, he was clearly unhappy about Roosevelt revealing the details about the coup. Alam dismissed Roosevelt's account as 'nonsense' and tried unsuccessfully to prevent its publication.

In Roosevelt's description of the events that led to the coup there is one point often discussed with regard to the BBC's role. When Roosevelt gives details of his meeting with the Shah he says since the Shah did not know him personally he tried to reassure the Shah of the validity of the coup operation, and the fact that he was representing the US President Eisenhower and British Prime Minister Churchill. He then tells the Shah that in case he does not believe what he is conveying he could listen to a broadcast of the BBC. 'Prime Minister Churchill has arranged to have a specific change made in the announcement on the BBC broadcast tomorrow night. Instead of saying it is now midnight the announcer will say it is now – pause – exactly midnight,' Roosevelt tells the Shah.[111]

Much has been made of this sentence as an indicator of how the BBC was used in the coup process.[112] A recent programme on Al Jazeera used it to explain the continuing mistrust of the British and seemingly to justify the attacks on the BBC by the Islamic Republic.[113] However, two points need to be borne in mind. First, this could not have been broadcast on the BBC Persian Service since Persian broadcasts ended long before midnight Iran time. This could, possibly, have been something considered for the BBC World Service that had from time to time been used to give British nationals overseas wartime or crisis-time coded messages. Thus it would not be unusual for the British government to use a coded message on a BBC broadcast to forewarn British nationals living abroad of a possible looming coup leading to crisis and chaos as a result of the downfall of Mossadeq. Second, the sentence that follows the above in Roosevelt's book is hardly quoted. It tells us the coded message was not necessary. 'The Shah pointed out that, having recognized me, he needed no such confirmation,' says Roosevelt.[114] Thus it is unlikely in the extreme that such a message was ever put out on the BBC broadcast. However, now that the documents of both the American and the British governments reveal how the officials of both countries refrained from giving the full facts and covered up the coup, it is hardly necessary to blow up this slight message reported by Roosevelt into an important document.

There is a far more convincing document of the Foreign Office, which reveals how the press and the BBC were misled after the coup.[115] This document spells out the line that officials should take in press conferences about the coup in Iran. The first instruction is to deny any first-hand knowledge and instead to say: 'Our information on Persia comes chiefly from monitored broadcasts and thus we had no prior knowledge of what happened.' The second instruction is to deny that the process was a coup: 'The word coup is inexact as a description of recent events.' Instead, the coup should be described in this way: 'The events of 19 August were due to a spontaneous popular uprising in favor of the Shah [...] other factors were violent dissatisfaction with the negative and dictatorial regime of Mossadeq.' The next instruction is to put the blame on the Soviet Union. 'The Tudeh were apparently contemplating a coup when forestalled by the August 19 rising,' the directive says.[116] Clearly this was the way the media, including the BBC, reported the events. Then came the finale: 'Persia needs immediate and substantial help to mend the economic chaos of the Mossadeq regime. Britain's aid can best come through an oil settlement [...] As regards to the form of settlement the proposals made in February by ourselves and the United States were the most generous settlement that we could devise and there is no reason to refuse to the new Prime Minister what we offered to Dr. Mossadeq.'[117]

The review of a recent book by Stephen Dorril on MI6 covert operations speaks of the operation in Iran as 'a more effective MI6 controlled coup'.[118] It says 'the coup removed the popular and moderate prime minister, Mohammed Mossadeq, despised by the British because he nationalized the Iranian oil industry. MI6 and the CIA armed, funded and directed the conspirators, and Mossadeq was ousted in 1953.'

On 26 August the Shah held a meeting with the American Ambassador in which he made an appeal for financial help: 'The figure the State department had in mind was US$36 million a year, in addition to military aid which amounts to about US$24 million.'[119] A few months later, the Shah accepted the renewal of the American military agreements that Mossadeq had refused to sign fearing loss of Iran's independence.[120] A total of US$65 million a year was recommended for defence support of Iran in November 1954.[121]

After the coup Winston Churchill wrote a letter (undated) to the Shah reminding him of the British support for his coming to power in 1942: 'Now that Mossadeq has gone, a solution of the Abadan problem and generally the oil dispute is possible, which would be agreeable both to Persian and British interests. We have no wish other than to see Persia prosperous but prosperity and prestige of a nation are rarely based upon forcible confiscation.'[122]

Fifty years on, the *Guardian* reporter in Tehran, Dan De Luce, wrote about the aftershocks of Operation Ajax in international relations. 'Ignoring international law, Britain and the US opted for the high-risk strategy of regime change in order to pre-empt a volatile enemy in the Middle East,' said De Luce. 'It was not Iraq, however, that was in the firing line but Iran, and the aftershocks are still being felt.'[123]

So, in this most crucial of political moments, when tension between Britain and Iran was at its most extreme, we see a somewhat confused policy in regard to the BBC Persian Service. On the one hand, written policy begins to note that subtle persuasion is preferable to overt propaganda, yet, in the next moment, the Service is under pressure to follow a strict diktat of information to be broadcast. We have noted the pressure felt by its Iranian employees, the majority of whom supported the general mood in Iran in favour of Mossadeq and in favour of oil nationalization; the overwhelming referendum is a clear index of that. Avoiding professional duties was their way of both acting politically at a distance from Tehran and putting distance between themselves and BBC content. It is also important to note the somewhat confused – and confusing – audience response to the Service. Despite popular hostility to Britain, audiences for the BBC remained high[124] and as we saw in the midst of the crisis people switched to the BBC to hear the news of the oil dispute. It left an indelible memory on the Persian psyche about the clandestine nature of British politics, creating notions of endless manipulation 'behind the curtain' ('*posht-e parde*'). It also left enduring confusion about the voice of the BBC Persian Service: was it independent or the voice of the master from London? The confusion remains to this day, as we shall see.

4

The BBC and the Iranian Revolution of 1979

While the Persian Service broadcasts daily through thick and thin, it is the moments of greatest controversy that are naturally the most interesting. Here we focus on the events leading up to and during the revolution that brought down the Pahlavi monarchy and turned Iran into a very particular kind of republic, a period in which the BBC was alleged to have played a very particular role. We try to show the actual role that the BBC played as well as the perceptions of its role by both Iranian and British players in this drama. We also explore again the ongoing dance between the FCO and the BBC regarding the influence of the former, and the credibility and autonomy of the latter.

In the early 1970s, the Shah was regarded internationally as an unrivalled and ambitious dictator and a devoted ally of the US, playing a crucial sub-imperial role within the region yet enjoying excellent relations with the international community. Iran was seen as enjoying prosperity and economic growth as the Shah staged the extravagant celebrations of the 2,500th anniversary of the Iranian monarchy at Persepolis in 1971. To avert political change, he introduced the so-called 'White Revolution', an ambitious programme of land reform, and set up his own political party, Rastakhiz, with compulsory membership and dues. Both of these created tension and dissent. During the late 1960s the Shah had become increasingly dependent on his secret police (SAVAK) in controlling those opposition movements critical of his reforms. With the combination of SAVAK monitoring of internal dissent and a vast army equipped with modern weaponry looking beyond its borders, in the mid-1970s the Shah's regime appeared durable. Despite endemic corruption and complex economic problems, it appeared that the regime was indestructible.

Even so, movements against the Shah were gathering momentum inside Iran and among Iranians abroad. These included armed uprisings and underground movements inside Iran as well as the political activities of the disenchanted clergy and the liberal nationalist movement, the National Front. The International Confederation of Iranian Students in Europe and the United States often organized successful demonstrations during the Shah's visits abroad and these served to unmask his claim to popularity. At the same time, the gradual rise in the price of oil throughout the 1970s, pushed by the Shah through the Organization of Petroleum Exporting Countries (OPEC), angered the West while the perilous state of human rights in Iran began to gain international attention.

OPEC ministers meeting in Tehran in December 1973 had put up the price of oil by over US$2 per barrel. Iran's oil income, which had risen from US$90 million in 1955 to US$1.1 billion by 1970, now soared to a staggering US$21.4 billion: 'The Shah revelled in the attention he attracted as the leader of the oil producing nations, pressing their claim to higher income.'[1] The US president Richard Nixon and the Secretary of State, Henry Kissinger, had tried without success to convince the Shah to reduce the price of oil since it was putting an undue burden on the world economy. The Shah was not convinced. He had by this stage become too powerful to even listen to what the US was saying: 'These bastard Americans,' the Shah told his chief of protocol Alam in March 1973, 'especially our friend Mr. Kissinger, must give up pretending that whatever they say has the authority of holy writ.'[2] The British had suggested an increase in several stages but the Shah had rejected that proposal too. The Anglo–American response was to block the sale of Iranian oil through sanctions. High oil prices and a crisis in the oil market eventually led to a reduction in fuel consumption, forcing OPEC members to reduce their output. Iranian oil revenue dropped over the years, causing shortages of funds and a halt to some of the Shah's ambitious development programmes, and causing tension in his hitherto problem-free relations with the Americans and the British. By 1976 some of the basic infrastructure sectors such as transport, education and power supply were almost entirely ignored. Across the country the inadequacy of housing, food supplies and basic services had led to havoc and outcry.

As early as June 1976 the Shah began complaining about the British press, including the BBC Persian Service. As Alam, the Shah's chief of protocol, describes it, the Shah was angry that *The Times* and the *Guardian* were accusing him of operating a police state and said that "'the BBC Persian programme has made similar allegations, saying Iran and Saudi Arabia could be denied access to Western military technology [...] What are the bloody fools on about," exclaimed the Shah, "tell the British ambassador that if his media and political bosses really feel this way, we shall be forced to reconsider our purchases of weapons from the UK."'[3] He had become so confident of his position that he threatened international powers and played one against the other.[4]

The Shah's fortunes changed in just over two years. A string of demonstrations, strikes and mass protests at home and protests abroad gained international attention. With the fall in oil exports even the Shah was forced to admit in January 1977 that the economy was in decline. 'We are broke,' he admitted to his chief of protocol Alam. 'Everything seems doomed to grind to a standstill and meanwhile many of the programmes we had planned must be postponed.'[5] The US president, Jimmy Carter, had unleashed a human rights campaign on Iran and military tribunals were instructed to revise procedure and to provide better facilities for political detainees. A Red Cross team had been sent to Iran and reported that 'one in three inmates had been tortured'.[6] Iran's intellectuals began to see the signs of crisis and took courage for the first time to discuss it in public by writing open letters. In August 1977, Jamshid Amouzegar was appointed Prime Minister, the Shah hoping that his appointment would improve the economic situation and overcome the crisis.

The BBC Persian Service, not hugely important for some time, rose to prominence during the period from 1977 to 1979. It began reporting the details of political developments even if they were anti-Shah. Iranians became avid listeners and, especially during the uprising of 1977 and 1978, the BBC expanded beyond the limited domain of intellectuals and the upper classes. People from different backgrounds listened to the BBC as it came to serve as a useful counterweight to the state-run radio and television network in Iran. BBC Persian Service broadcasts became a trusted medium for news and information for Iranians at home and in the diaspora mainly because it was the medium through which the voices of opposition could be frequently heard.

As such, during 1977–8, the BBC became a major thorn in the side of British relations with Iran. The Shah eventually described the BBC as his 'number one enemy'.[7] Through his meetings with the British ambassador in Tehran, Anthony Parsons, through messages carried by the Iranian ambassador in London, Parviz Radji, and by sending several high-level delegations – including his sister Princess Ashraf – from Tehran to London, the Shah made known his complaints about the BBC to Downing Street and the FCO.

Anthony Parsons wrote regularly to the FCO about the Shah's complaints, going as far as to question the viability of the BBC, given that it was having such an adverse effect on British relations with one of its most trusted allies. As early as 30 June 1976, Parsons began giving warnings about the Shah's concerns. The first came when, according to the Shah, the BBC Persian Service had broadcast the summary of a survey on Iran in the *Financial Times*, 'drawing heavily on its negative aspects'.[8] 'What was the BBC Persian Service trying to achieve?' the Shah asked. This, according to the Shah, 'was damaging British interests in Iran'.[9] A copy of Parsons' telegram was sent to the BBC while Parsons noted that he had repeated to the Shah the point about the 'independence of the BBC'.[10] Nicholas Barrington of the Foreign Office asked the BBC's head of the Eastern Service, Mark Dodd, to look into the complaint.[11] Having looked at the piece, Mark Dodd told Barrington in a telephone conversation that 'although in stylistic terms our rendering of the article might seem a little clumsy here and there, this was largely due to the fact that it had to be translated back from Farsi into English. Its content seemed to me very fair.'[12]

Parsons appeared to adopt the Shah's attitude that BBC Persian broadcasts were in fact perceived as the publicly expressed viewpoint of the British government. In another report Parsons warned that 'we only succeed in damaging our interests if we adopt public attitudes which are at variance with our policies'.[13] Most of the telegrams now in the public domain reveal that he supported the Shah, viewed the BBC as having little real influence in Iran and, as such, considered it relatively unimportant for effecting British foreign policy. In one, he said that he regarded the Persian Service of the BBC as 'very largely a waste of time and money',[14] and added that he scarcely met any Persians who listened to it and that, if they did, they regarded it with suspicion. Parsons repeated his disbelief that the Persian Service 'does a positive service to British interests in Iran'.[15]

The FCO repeatedly challenged Parsons' position. Nicholas Barrington, from the Guidance and Information Department at FCO, wrote back to him: 'I hope you don't mind my saying that I was slightly surprised by the strength and monolithic nature of your views.'[16] He argued that the BBC would see in them an example of 'the FCO's concern with short term expediency which they find inhibiting to much longer term aims'. Barrington explained that the rationale behind foreign-language broadcasting was 'to operate in the medium and long term, influencing those who may one day form an alternative government'. He asked: 'Is there not some national interest [in making Iranians] accustomed and sympathetic to Western democratic traditions, particularly when the opposition has no local voice?'[17]

There were, however, clear differences of approach within the FCO. A 'confidential' account of the minutes of the BBC Board of Governors meeting held in July 1976 confirms that, for the first time, the FCO was actually considering abolishing the BBC Persian Service under mounting pressure from Iran:

> The Shah's objections had led to exchanges between the British Ambassador in Tehran and the FCO, as a result of which the FCO had set up a small official working party to see whether the Persian Service should be altered or abolished. This was the first time in the Director-General's experience that the FCO had seemed prepared to consider altering or abolishing a language service because it was causing embarrassment.[18]

The working party was to consider whether the Persian Service 'should be altered in any way or abolished altogether'.[19] On 15 July 1976, M. Kendall of the Guidance and Information Department at the FCO, who was asked to conduct the review, wrote to the BBC's head of the Eastern Service, Mark Dodd, spelling out the terms of reference for the review of the service: 'To examine the benefit to the [British] national interest of the Persian Service of the BBC as an instrument in the overseas information programme and to make recommendations for its continuation, modification or abolition.'[20] In submitting the terms of reference, the FCO clarified that the use of 'national interest' had been taken deliberately from the Licence and Agreement, since that and no other document expressed the BBC's 'constitutional requirements'.[21] The Licence and Agreement was written on 7 July 1969 and has, as its final phrase, the reference to 'national interest':

> The Corporation shall consult and collaborate with the Department so specified and shall obtain and accept from them such information regarding conditions in and the policies of HMG aforesaid towards, the countries so prescribed and other countries as will

enable the Corporation to plan and prepare its programmes in the External Services in the national interest.[22]

Put simply, BBC External Services should consult with the relevant FCO department on matters that could affect British national interests. However, the BBC was also pushing for its own expertise in design and production of its programmes. When the views of Anthony Parsons were sent to Mark Dodd in 1976, he responded with anger, saying that 'assaults' on the Persian Service from the British Embassy in Tehran were 'nothing new'.[23] Dodd said he was at a loss to know what Sir Anthony meant by saying that the 'Persian Service tends to be regarded as propaganda' and asks 'propaganda for whom?' Dodd then criticized the ambassador directly:

> The term in which Parsons discusses the BBC's role suggests that he has no understanding or appreciation of the nature of broad-casting. He seems to measure its effectiveness as, in the first place, an agency source for newspapers and, in the second, by its ability to reach a very narrowly defined elite [...] It must be evident to the FCO that the sort of Persian Service that Parsons advocates would be nonsense.[24]

Parsons was advocating a Persian Service that would report mainly on business and trade and not become too involved in politics, while Dodd argued that 'commercially orientated programmes can only live within the structure of an overall Service'.[25] He argued that without the news and current affairs, he doubted if anyone would listen to Bazaar-o-Bourse, the business news programme of the Service.[26]

This spat seems to have followed a visit to London in June 1976 by Princess Ashraf, the twin of the Shah and the most powerful member of his family.[27] She had a ten-minute 'private conversation' with the then prime minister, James Callaghan, and brought a message of 'continuing concern' from the Shah about 'the attitude of the press and the BBC towards Iran'. Callaghan actually agreed in the meeting that the coverage of Iran had been 'deplorable', but said there was very little he could do to influence the British press. Ashraf asked whether it was not the case that the BBC was 'owned' by the government and expressed great surprise that it could not simply be controlled by the government. The Prime Minister explained that the relationship with the BBC overseas services was a 'complicated' one, but that the extent of government influence was 'very strictly limited'.[28]

The Shah consistently made reference to the staff of the BBC Persian Service. 'Could it be that Iranian dissidents in the BBC were distorting scripts?' he asked Parsons as early as June 1976.[29] After several reviews of the Persian Service by the designated board, H.D. Lancashire compiled the final results in November 1977.[30] Here the issues that had been raised over the previous two years were tackled so as to clarify the role of the BBC's language services in general, and the Persian Service in particular, in securing long-term British interests around the world. The paper quotes a lecture by Gerard Mansell, the Managing Director of the BBC External Services, in which he states that the questions about the future of BBC external broadcasting must rest not just on issues of 'narrowly conceived self interest', but more on the importance Britain attaches to the 'free movement of ideas and the worldwide dissemination of truth'. The review panel concluded that the BBC could retain its standing and repute only by retaining its 'credibility' with listeners, and that credibility 'rests on accurate and unbiased news and fair and consistent analysis and comment'.[31]

Clearly, the review panel believed that any short-term interests were of lesser importance than such a long-term view.[32] It argued that Iran was a country of considerable strategic importance and it could be assumed that the Shah would not remain its only ruler, and that therefore Britain must consider the variety of views to be found in Iran. The panel accepted that under the circumstances it was inevitable that the truth might irritate the Shah and cause trouble for the Ambassador, but stipulated that the long-term aims of the BBC should not be compromised.[33] They took account of all the points made by Ambassador Parsons about bilateral relationships, but came to the conclusion that 'the longer term power for influence of the BBC is a valuable asset which should not be surrendered so long as funds are available to continue it'.[34] This review made a powerful defence of the international importance of the BBC in conveying British values and the acknowledgement that its credibility was based on providing a truthful account of events; it became the blueprint for the defence of the BBC's independence. It rejected Parsons' call for closure or reduction of the Service. However, it did not mean that the FCO did not have the right to express concerns when it felt that the British 'national interest' was threatened.

The Shah was not mollified and continued to relay his dissatisfaction to Anthony Parsons. Such was the imagined power of BBC broadcasts that the Shah related them directly to the continued UK relations with Iran. The Shah's strong objections were relayed to London and the FCO in turn asked Parsons to convey to the Shah that his complaints had been taken up with the BBC. Several meetings took place between the FCO, the BBC and the Iranian ambassador in London, while the official British policy was that it was best for the Iranian ambassador to raise the complaints directly with the BBC. The Iranian ambassador in London, Parviz Radji, catalogued the various meetings he had with Mansell and Dodd as well as with Ian Trethowan, the Director-General of the BBC. It is clear from these accounts that the Shah frequently expressed his anger with the BBC Persian Service by cable.[35] The Iranian press also monitored BBC Persian Service output and noted its language. For example, on 15 December 1977, the newspaper *Keyhan International* published a list of what it ridiculed as BBC-esque reporting.[36] The article's headline was 'BBC's "surprises" touch a new low in journalism'. It criticized the general tone of the BBC giving less importance to the Shah during his visit to Washington and his meetings with the US president Jimmy Carter, and instead devoting more time to the anti-Shah demonstrations outside. It objected to the use of words such as 'guerrillas' for what Iran thought were 'terrorists' (a reference to the Fadayan-e Khalgh and Mojaheddin-e

Khalgh opposition groups). It ridiculed BBC Persian reporting that said 'thousands of Iranian students' gathered to enhance the cause of 'human rights'. It objected also to the fact that the BBC quoted an Amnesty International report on Iran without highlighting improvements that had been pointed to in the report. *Keyhan* concluded that BBC activities could not be considered 'accidental' since the department was under the 'direct supervision' of the British Foreign Office. It wondered why, when the two governments are friendly, 'the BBC is actively propagating violence in our country'. Mark Dodd defended the reporting in a letter to the BBC correspondent in Tehran, Andrew Whitley.[37] He said he had searched through the output of the Service and 'the Persian Service coverage of the Shah's arrival at the White House was drawn largely from dispatches of BBC correspondents in Washington, whose material was used by domestic services as well as elsewhere in the external services'. He presented facts and figures from the report negating the complaints in *Keyhan* and concluded that: 'in so many instances the *Keyhan* article grossly distorts what the Persian Service has actually broadcast'. Yet, in the same letter, Dodd stated that he is open to criticism and knows that the BBC 'cannot claim to get it right all the time'.[38]

On 24 January 1978, Ambassador Parsons had an audience with the Shah about the BBC, in order to explain the government's 'limitations in influencing the BBC and the damage which would be done if we crossed this line'.[39] The Shah remained unimpressed and accused the British government of having no interest in Iran 'except in terms of making money'. The Shah complained that ministers used to say nice things to him in private but that it had been 'a long time since anyone had the courage to say the same things in public'. He finished by asking Parsons to tell London that the 'BBC had brought us to the limit' and that if things did not get any better 'it would be impossible for our relationship to remain undamaged'.[40]

By the end of January 1978, Iran had filed a set of specific complaints against various BBC TV programmes, as well as David Dimbleby's interview with President Carter in which he accused Iran of human rights violations, Andrew Whitley's report for the *Financial Times* and human rights reports by Amnesty International. However, the BBC Persian Service remained, in their view, the main culprit.

Matters became more serious as the Persian broadcasts of the BBC became more popular in Iran over the following months. But why was it that the Persian Service that had been relatively unimportant in the 1960s and early 1970s had suddenly become the main source of information on developments inside Iran and among the exiled opposition? The Persian Service's senior programme assistant, Lutfali Khonji, recalls how during the 1960s there were no anti-Shah reports and only very widely reported news such as the Iranian students' anti-Shah demonstrations in Berlin would be covered. He also recalls how the Shah's birthdays would always be marked by playing the Iranian national anthem. However, according to Khonji, with major political events taking shape in Iran from the mid-1970s, the BBC Persian Service rose up to its journalistic task and there was no conspiracy:

> At this stage there was a lot to report since the opposition was gathering momentum and they were contacting us in the BBC with news. It was not just the Islamic activists but also the National Front and left activists of a variety of colors. They would call us daily giving us details of demonstrations, gatherings and their political statements. So we had a lot to report.[41]

Interestingly, some British voices began to raise the alarm about the role of the BBC. David Ransom, writing in the *Daily Telegraph* on 3 January 1978, asserted that the BBC Persian Service had been 'infiltrated by anti-Shah elements'.[42] But the Managing Director of BBC External Broadcasting, Gerard Mansell, strongly refuted this, accusing the *Daily Telegraph* of publishing views that are 'wholly without foundation'. Referring to several such opinions previously published in the paper, he said that they were merely 'repeating malicious accusations made over the weeks and months by those who have an interest in the news being manipulated for political ends'. He defended the staff in the Persian

Service as constituting a team of 'high quality' with 'impeccable professionalism' who had at no time given grounds for suspecting their integrity despite 'the pressures to which they, too, have been exposed'.[43]

Mansell wrote a similar letter to Peter Temple Morris, MP, who had received complaints about a member of the BBC Persian Service staff, providing details of the background and education of staff in the Persian Service.[44] Mansell notes that nine programme assistants in the Service had 'outstanding academic qualifications', with one holding a 'PhD in linguistics from London University'. There are similar letters from the Persian Programme Organizer, John Dunn, and other internal BBC exchanges responding to complaints, evidence of a strong campaign against the BBC Persian Service.[45] There are also several exchanges between the FCO and the BBC about Persian Service broadcasters. The Iranian government accused them of giving only 'the opposition side of the story', inviting the public to unrest and thus giving 'little importance to a balanced account of events'.[46]

Lutfali Khonji believed that this may have been the impression that was given, but that, in reality, a revolutionary movement was growing and everyone, including the staff of the Persian Service, had become far more involved in politics.[47] Political activists without access to the media in Iran were contacting the BBC with news (a process that by 2006 had its own name, crowdsourcing). According to Khonji:

> Those working in the BBC had their own set of contacts. Some had close contacts with Islamic scholars and activists. I was the main link for the National Front and as such my friends would pass on the relevant news on developments. Improved communications techniques meant that the BBC could be heard far better in Europe [...] and the Iranian diaspora were increasingly involved in the struggle for democracy in Iran. Another element that increased news coverage was that the BBC dispatched several reporters to Iran and thus could report from various corners of the country on developments. That meant the volume of incoming news was

suddenly drastically increased. New methods of broadcasting such as interviews were allowed.[48]

Another Persian broadcaster, Baqer Moin, acknowledged in a Radio 4 *Document* programme that he had been pro-revolution.[49] However, he added that BBC guidelines did not allow any of the broadcasters to bring their political opinions into their reporting. Moin, who became the head of the Persian Service in 1990, said that during the years leading to the revolution of 1979 there was little any individual broadcaster could do since most news and reports were prepared in the central newsroom, and were only translated and read by the broadcasters. Several reviews of the Persian Service suggest that as a rule this is an accurate description of the process. However, there were exceptions. Most found only small criticism in the production and delivery of news. One of the letters from the Embassy in Tehran to the Middle East Department of the FCO offers an example. It claimed that the report sent by the BBC British correspondent in Tehran, Andrew Whitley, was later edited in the Persian Service and that stories were added that had not originated from Whitley in Tehran.[50]

During this period, Andrew Whitley was under constant pressure. British and Iranian officials alike instructed him on how he should practise journalism. The Iranian information minister, Dariush Homayoun, told him that his first responsibility as a BBC journalist was 'to contribute towards greater Irano–British understanding' and that he should always 'be careful to see news against this wider background'.[51] Whitley's response was that perhaps Iran's officials should provide more information so reporters didn't always have to talk to the opposition.[52] In a separate letter Whitley illustrates how he was forced to explain his reports to British officials too:

> After Buckmaster's telephone call I discussed the situation with the Acting Head of Eastern Service who arranged for me to call at the FCO in the afternoon to present our case and the relevant documents to him. Another senior official also attended the meeting – I believe named Mike Carver. It was cordial, though it was made

quite clear to me how seriously the FCO regard the complaint and the Ambassador's telegram. Our right to broadcast the dispatch in Persian was accepted and I believe understood.[53]

The fact that Whitley had to meet so many times with the FCO to 'explain' and that FCO officials recommended that certain phrases could have been 'omitted' indicates that direct demands were being made by the FCO about the details of broadcasting. From the correspondence it also appears that some form of verbal agreement had been reached in the meetings between the BBC and the FCO over matters relating to the 'national interest'. In a letter marked 'personal and confidential', written on 19 April 1978, John Leahy, Assistant Under-Secretary responsible for information matters at the FCO, reminded Mansell of an agreement:

> You and I agreed the other day that there might be occasions when it would be right for me to send you papers which were intended for your eyes only [...] I should of course be happy to come and discuss with you [...] ways for establishing closer supervision of the Persian Service and if possible, reducing its commentaries on Iranian internal affairs to, say, five minutes at a time.[54]

There is also evidence that in 1978 the FCO tried to interfere in the BBC World Service's process of recruiting a correspondent for Iran. In several exchanges, the FCO expressed dismay at the BBC's appointment of a Mr Branigan from the *Washington Post* and also considered it unacceptable that Liz Thurgood of the *Guardian* should replace Andrew Whitley while he went on leave. The basic argument made was that the Shah of Iran had strongly objected to reports by both and they are 'heartily disliked'.[55]

The Shah, who had always harboured suspicions of the British, felt that BBC broadcasts reflected the British government's anger over failed negotiations over oil prices. In his meeting with the US ambassador, William Sullivan, in August 1978 the Shah connected BBC broadcasts to the issue of oil negotiations between the UK and Iran, saying that it gave 'the British antagonists all the excuses they needed to attempt the resumption of their ancient subversions in Iran.'[56] The Shah was aware that the increase in the price of oil during the early 1970s had triggered the Anglo–American hostility towards him and felt this was related to the uprising against him. In August 1978, when the Shah was talking to Ambassador Sullivan,[57] the political turmoil had reached a new height. The Shah burst out with fury in his meeting and for nearly ten minutes, Sullivan recalls, the Shah related incident after incident that had taken place in the country, each one constituting an assault on his government's authority. Sullivan reports that what bothered the Shah was that 'this intrigue went beyond the capabilities of the Soviet KGB and must therefore involve the British and the American CIA [...] listening to the BBC broadcasts that were critical of his government confirmed him in his analysis.'[58]

By September 1978 the Shah had changed prime minister three times but none had been able to control the unfolding revolution. Moreover, a host of international journalists had come to Tehran and were interviewing opposition politicians and activists. Hedayatullah Matin Daftari recalls that this was the first time he heard slogans demanding an Islamic Republic. He recalls that Andrew Whitley and Richard Oppenheimer of the BBC used to interview him regularly, and that he used to pass on all proclamations and statements from the oppositional Freedom Movement proclamations and statements to them. He blames the Shah for censoring the internal media to such an extent that 'people had no other means of getting information about the political developments'. This, according to Matin Daftari, had left a big gap, which the BBC was filling efficiently. Most people used to listen to the BBC as if it were a religious duty, he says: 'Everyone would stop all they were doing and listen to the BBC to get the latest news and developments.' He recalls how once during a trip to northern Iran, the taxi driver stopped the car, apologized and said he had to listen to the BBC.[59]

On 21 September, when Ambassador Parsons went to visit Prime Minister Jafar Sharif-Emami, he reported to the FCO that the message conveyed by Sharif-Emami was even more somber than the ones from the Shah. Sharif-Emami told Parsons that the tone of BBC broadcasts were such that all who listened were convinced that 'the BBC's sympathies lay with those who wanted to overthrow the Shah'. Sharif-Emami said that other broadcasters were putting out 'balanced or non-committal' accounts of events in Iran whereas the BBC 'were contributing to the sporadic disturbances' that were happening. 'There was a higher incidence of these disturbances immediately after BBC broadcasts,' according to the Prime Minister. He directly accused the BBC broadcasts of having a 'destabilizing effect'. He suggested a change of staff at the BBC Persian Service: 'It is of course difficult to ask the BBC to change its tone without unacceptable staff changes but there is no doubt that the BBC is having the effect of seriously misleading the public about the HMG attitude.' He also complained that the BBC had 'diluted' the message of support for the Shah by Prime Minister Callaghan. In the same report the British Ambassador speaks of Andrew Whitley's reports from Tehran as being less objective than Reuters, referring to him as 'a very inexperienced journalist' who is under the influence of 'an anti-Shah group of foreign journalists'.[60]

The last three months of 1978

In the last three months before the revolution a few important things changed. First, Ayatollah Khomeini moved in October 1978 from Najaf, Iraq, where the Shah had had him exiled, to Paris, France. Here his access to the international media, including the BBC Persian Service, was greatly enhanced. 'During the 105 days he gave 132 interviews: a remarkable rate of activity for a man in his eighth decade,' remarked John Simpson of the BBC who had gone over to France to interview Khomeini.[61] Describing the scene in Le Café des Trois Communes, near Khomeini's residence, Simpson says:

> For sixteen weeks, from October 1978 to the following January, this café had been the operations centre for the journalists and

camera crew who had gathered in Neauphle le Chateau to report the exotic presence in this small unremarkable village of Ayatollah Haji Sayyed Ruhollah Mussavi Khomeini, and his return from exile to triumph in Iran. Neauphle le Chateau was not entirely unaccustomed to fame: Brigitte Bardot had once lived here but it had never seen anything like the thousands of enthusiastic Iranians who flooded in to join their leader.[62]

Cassettes of his sermons and his interviews were produced daily and sent to Iran.[63] A close aid, the Iranian lawyer Ahmad Salamatian, recalls how these cassettes were prepared and what their immediate impact was in Iran:

> An activist who worked closely with Khomeini, known as Ringo, told us that in Iraq they sent Khomeini's speeches to Iran by playing them over the phone. He suggested that in order to send these in such a way as to miss the Iranian interception, they would have to be shorter than four minutes. Then we managed to find some Sony tape condensers that would reduce his 20-minute speeches to just less than four minutes. We had three sets of these condensers and were constantly sending his sermons to Tehran. His cassettes were so popular that most shops across Iran were constantly busy copying and selling Khomeini cassettes.[64]

Through his interviews Khomeini was on all major international television and radio stations, and pages of press were devoted to analysing his messages for the downfall of the Shah.

Second, and in contrast, the Shah appeared progressively more unwell from mid-September onwards. European and American ambassadors meeting the Shah in person reported back to their governments with concern about how the Shah was losing power, and looking and sounding weak and confused. It was precisely through these months that the news of the Shah's illness was being reported in diplomatic circles. Anthony Parsons writes of his long audience with the Shah on 10 October when 'he looked haggard and his mood was grim.'[65] In fact, reports of rumours about the Shah's illness had been trickling in since August. These started when the Shah had been unable to complete a visit to the southern port of Bandar Abbas because of an illness, when 'he did not appear to be in a particularly good shape on a number of subsequent public occasions'.[66] In July, when the Shah had gone to the Caspian for his usual summer holidays, the Embassy reported that he had not been seen at all in public: 'People began to say that his health was deteriorating even further'.[67] The *Guardian* also carried a report about his suspected illness.[68] This meant that key international political players were weighing their options more seriously than before. There were serious differences of opinion between the British, the American and the French about what to do in case the Shah was to find it impossible to cope.[69]

Third, as a consequence of the above, international leaders had begun discussing either a more active role for the army or the formation of a regency council as possible options to stop the Shah's regime from falling. Therefore, for the first time the inability of the Shah to cope had become a serious reality. The power of daily directives from Ayatollah Khomeini, now stationed in Neauphle le Chateau and increasingly looking like the main leader of the revolution, could tilt the balance against the Shah. Yet, in the last three months, the BBC Persian Service carried his messages in its daily news and current affairs programmes heard by millions of Iranians. It also debated and analysed the international community's concerns, as would be expected from a serious broadcaster. BBC Persian broadcasts had become available on shortwave, which meant that the Iranian diaspora could also listen across the world. And international media, which had found direct access to Khomeini in the heart of Europe, were discussing on a daily basis his vision, his ideology and his stature as a Gandhi-like leader with millions of followers obeying his edicts on how to topple the Shah.

It was during these final three months that the confrontation with the BBC seems to have come to a head. Although the media around the world was reporting the same news about political development in Iran, the BBC Persian Service was singled out for blame. This was partly due to the Shah's paranoia about Britain and the memory of how his father was removed from power. He also remembered the role BBC Persian broadcasts had played during the oil nationalization and his own return to Iran in 1953 after the Anglo–American coup that toppled the democratically elected Prime Minister Mossadeq. Another source of anxiety for the Shah was the BBC's direct contacts with the opposition. For the first time people in Iran could hear the views of the opposition directly through their interviews and statements woven into news bulletins.

'Popular opinion is riveted on Khomeini himself – who has now left Iraq for Paris,' wrote Anthony Parsons from Tehran: 'The Prime Minister has claimed privately that the return of Khomeini could plunge the country into civil war.' In his view, although it was doubtful that the Iranian people wanted a theocratic state, popular support for Khomeini had reached the point where 'any agreement with the more moderate clergy may not be enough'. Moreover, although 'the Iranian armed forces owe so much to the Pahlavis, it is not certain that they would stick with the Shah's commitment to liberalization'.[70] Indeed, a military prime minister, General Azhari, had been appointed by the Shah on the recommendation of the Americans in a last-minute attempt to quell the course of events. The nightly BBC Persian programmes angered him. While daily demonstrations and strikes were bringing the government to its knees, General Azhari singled out the BBC Persian Service for blame. On 12 November, Iranian authorities jammed the BBC Persian Service.[71] A contact in the National Iranian Radio and Television (NIRT) told Andrew Whitely: 'NIRT have made three frequency changes in order to jam the BBC Persian Service.' In order to counter this jamming the BBC then switched to broadcasting from two additional transmitters in Cyprus and three additional transmitters in the UK.[72] A further attempt at jamming was made by the Iranian army, which had instructed NIRT to broadcast a programme over the BBC medium-wave transmission: 'Their intention in the future is to use a typical jamming noise to blot out the 213 MW transmission using the powerful

NIRT transmitter in Tehran, Ahwaz and Abadan.'[73] There are notable parallels with the post-2009 period, when again the BBC – although television this time, not radio – bore much of the brunt of Iranian ire and when jamming was – and continues to be – the tool to prevent Iranians themselves from watching and listening.

It was not just the BBC that was being jammed. On 27 November the military government's intolerance of the media was in full sway. 'There is virtually no local press and the TV/radio is heavily censored,' wrote Ambassador Parsons from Tehran: 'Hence the only way in which the opposition, including Khomeini, the National Front and the religious leaders could be heard is through the BBC Persian Service.' The whole country was therefore 'glued to the Persian Service every evening'. The British Ambassador felt there was 'no doubt that yesterday's general strike [25 November] would not have been nearly so widespread had it not been for its advance dissemination over the Persian Service'. He argued that it was against this background that the military authorities in Iran regarded the Persian Service to be 'an important contribution to their present security problem throughout the country'.[74]

Telegram after telegram from the Ambassador's files detail Iran's complaints in the last three months of 1978. 'The BBC problem which has been simmering briskly for months has now boiled over,' reports Parsons, conveying the Iranian threat that 'unless there was an improvement on the part of the BBC, there would be retaliation', including the possibility of the withdrawal of their ambassador from London.[75]

On 28 November, tension escalated further when the British Ambassador went to see General Azhari. He reported to the FCO and the Cabinet Office that 'the BBC occupied much of our time', and General Azhari had warned that he had no choice but to announce that:

> The BBC was a mouthpiece of the HMG and that HMG were therefore behind the opposition and the disturbances in Iran.

He asked me to tell my government that the BBC was creating more trouble for Iran than the Soviet Government [...] He said he would welcome all journalists to his office except for those that had connections with the BBC.[76]

The following day Parsons reported the text of the anti-BBC broadcasts on NIRT radio.

The more trouble there is, the more the BBC likes it [...] why does the BBC consider that the internal affairs of Iran have anything to do with it [...] the BBC is a rumourmonger, it is producing a lot of false reporting while claiming to be impartial [...] why does it keep saying 'unconfirmed reports' in its broadcasts? The BBC is calling for resistance [...] cashing in on people's uneasiness [...] behind the BBC broadcast lays the face of black colonialism.[77]

But BBC reporting did not subside with these pressures. Parsons wrote with another unspecified warning on 3 December. He said the Iranian Foreign Minister had contacted him saying he had heard the Persian Service would broadcast a statement by Khomeini on shortwave transmissions 19 and 25 metres. He said he had been asked to stop this broadcast otherwise 'there will be a very drastic reaction indeed against HMG'.[78] In a subsequent telegram he said that the German Ambassador had told him that they had 'stopped Deutsche Welle from carrying Khomeini's declaration'.[79]

In December 1978, Ambassador Radji wrote to Sir Michael Swann, Chairman of the BBC Board of Governors, accusing the Persian Section of 'a positively hostile attitude towards Iran during the past two years'. He claimed that the Persian Section pursued 'methods of journalistic manipulation' and 'doctoring of the news', adding that the BBC was careful 'to cover its tracks in a strictly legal sense by creating an aura of supposed objectivity', which could have been an interesting critique of BBC practice were it made in a different tone. To illustrate his point, he said that the BBC Home Service, World Service and television all reported the ending of oil strikes in the south of Iran, but that the Persian

Service refused to do so and instead reported the continuation of the strike. He also argued that the Persian Section 'consistently' used sources that were 'hostile to the Iranian regime'.[80]

One of the common complaints voiced by the Shah's supporters was that the BBC was always ahead of the news in Iran and that, in particular, the BBC would announce upcoming demonstrations before they were announced in Iran. This comes up in the letter of complaint from Ambassador Radji, who accused the Section of violating 'journalistic ethics':

> No responsible radio or newspaper carries news of wildcat strikes in advance. But the Section does so as a matter of policy. For a whole week it tells its listeners that a strike will be observed on a specific day.[81]

He goes on to say that the Section ignores 'the fact that the Khomeini-led part of the opposition' is for the overthrow of the regime and thus illegal. Radji compared the coverage to the BBC regularly interviewing the IRA or the British Anarchist Party, saying that he had never seen the British media publicizing in advance demonstrations by the IRA and thus accusing the BBC of 'double standards'. He also criticized the technical aspects of reporting such as sourcing, language and translation. For example, he says, the sentence 'students were asked to leave the campus' was translated as 'students were ordered to get lost by the troops'. It was argued that 'differences of syntax, cadence and style between English and Persian provide ample opportunity for twisting news items or comments used through translation'. Radji concluded that the BBC followed a policy of 'deliberate hostility towards Iran' with the effect of 'subversion of Iran's legally consti-tuted Government and systematic encouragement of violence'.[82]

Although, in his telegram to the Foreign Office, Parsons described this as a 'virulent' attack on the BBC,[83] he considered the main objection by the Shah to be 'the extensive and over sympathetic coverage given to the dissidents and students' and a refusal to report 'improvements' in human rights. He also felt that he could and should intervene directly by speaking to the BBC reporter in Tehran, Andrew Whitley, and to the assistant head of the Eastern Service, David Stride:

> I told them that, although I considered it none of my business what they choose to report, they should know just how unpopular the BBC was now with the Shah. I told them that if the clock were turned back four years to when Bierman was expelled, Whitley would have been out of the country by now. Whitley accepted that he had filed a few dispatches that had been critical of the Government's role in the disturbances but said he had also recently filed a number of favorable stories, e.g. about a state visit to Oman.[84]

The Ambassador's veiled threats echoed those of Iranian officials. In a letter to the FCO, Parsons enclosed an aide memoir from the Foreign Ministry in Iran, which ran: 'In spite of repeated warnings [to the British government in recent months covering] the malicious policy of the BBC Farsi programme [...] no changes have unfortunately been made in the policy.' It considered that since the corporation is not a private organization and that the British government provides its budget, 'the excuse that the BBC is independent of the Government' is 'unacceptable'. It argued that the BBC seems to be a 'propaganda instrument for those groups whose aim is to encourage people to revolt against the legally established regime of Iran' and this was 'against the mutual interests of the two nations'.[85] Two main cases were identified. One was a report read by Baqer Moin in the main flagship programme *Jame Jahan Nama* and the other an interview with Ayatollah Khomeini that was broadcast in the same programme.

The report found to be objectionable was translated by the Embassy in Tehran and attached:

> Religious and political leaders of Iran have requested that tomorrow, Sunday, be announced as a protest and mourning day. A BBC reporter in Tehran says in his report: the speaker of one of the important religious leaders in Mashad said that people demonstrated inside the Shrine of Imam Reza which is the holiest

religious place for the Shiite followers of the world. He said soldiers attacked and shot them with automatic rifles. Two religious leaders of Mashad, who are amongst the most prominent sources of the Shiite sect, Ayatollah Shirazi and Ayatollah Ghomi issued communiqués in which they protested against the shooting [...] and urged a one day national mourning on Sunday. Today Ayatollah Khomeini requested that a one-day strike be made as a gesture instead. Meanwhile several other religious leaders in Tehran asked for a one-day mourning which practically means a strike. Ayatollah Khomeini's communiqué coincided with the National Front communiqué. The National Front in its communiqué, which is very proactive, says the Government has shown its anti-Islamic face.[86]

This broadcast could be said to be somewhat different from the usual style of BBC reporting. The name of the BBC reporter in Tehran is not given, so it is difficult to know whether this was Andrew Whitley's piece translated by Baqer Moin or whether parts had been added to the report from other sources. During the months of protests leading up to the revolution, the BBC Persian Service was receiving information from many Iranian contacts such as the National Front and a variety of sources close to the prominent clergy in Iran – and these could have been added to the main report. It also does not say to whom the comments from the ayatollahs were addressed, nor whether by interview or in a statement. It says 'several religious leaders' had said the same thing, without naming or quoting them. This report – if translated accurately – does appear more editorialized than usual BBC reports and many BBC editors might not have agreed with a broadcast in that tone.

In a controversial interview with the BBC a few months after the Iranian Revolution of 1979, Lord George Brown, the former Labour Foreign Secretary, distinguished the BBC World Service in English from the language services and targeted the émigré broadcasters as the source of the problem, rather than those on the ground in Tehran:

You have the separate band – separate broadcasts – in the languages of the people in the country which deal with the political issues [...] which is staffed by – necessarily so – émigrés, refugees from those countries who are hostile to the regime of the country; that is why they are émigrés in the first place. They are operating in a way that expresses their views, their desires, which may or may not fit with the policy of the Government of this country. And because the Government funds the BBC – and everyone overseas knows this – it is assumed that this is British Government policy.[87]

In the *Daily Telegraph* of December 1978, Julian Amery, MP, picked up the same theme, arguing that 'the young radicals have achieved an effective penetration of the Iranian Service of the BBC'.[88] Lord George Brown had made an even stronger accusation, saying that during November 1978 and again in January 1979, when he was directly involved and knew what the British foreign policy was and had daily contact with the British embassy, he knew that the 'Farsi service run by émigré Iranians' was not only 'putting out anti-Shah propaganda', but it was putting out 'heavily pro-Khomeini propaganda', neither of which – according to him – was British government policy. Brown claimed that 'one of his (Khomeini) associates on the staff of the BBC Overseas Service put out a call to the people of Tehran to riot, to go to the streets' and 'that was going beyond reporting news', and actually called for a 'parliamentary inquiry' to determine whether or not 'this very thin line between propaganda and news, between propaganda and truth, was not overstepped'.[89] He had made the same claim in November 1978 in the *Sunday Express* where he accused the BBC of 'putting out heavy pro-Khomeini propaganda'.[90]

Gerard Mansell of the BBC responded with equal force: 'I am going to be equally forthright and say that this is utter rubbish. Indeed I am surprised that Lord George Brown should have allowed himself to lend his name to denigration of this kind.'[91] Mansell believed that Brown had 'his ear bent by people who had an interest in doing so' and wondered why he hadn't 'checked his facts' with the BBC. He issued an invitation to Brown to listen to 'all the recordings of our Persian Service output'. Mansell's strong defence of the performance of the Persian Service, which was published in *Broadcast*, the internal BBC magazine, on 11 December 1978, concluded: 'all this about the BBC Persian Service helping to destabilize Iran on behalf of that elderly exile, the Ayatollah Khomeini, is of course nonsense'.[92] In a direct letter to John Junor, the *Sunday Express* Editor, Mansell had said that the external services of the BBC did not 'transmit propaganda, either in Persian or any other language', nor were they compliant in serving the cause of the Shah's exiled religious opponents or anyone else:

> Over the period of May to October [1978] there were more than 450 items on developments in Iran in our Persian Service news output. Only six of those quoted the Ayatollah. Extracts from interviews given by the Ayatollah to the British TV and Radio were broadcast only once – and then for sound journalistic reasons. They were hardly calculated to foment civil strife but any Iranian can buy cassette recordings of the Ayatollah's outpourings in the bazaar. These are nothing to do with the BBC.[93]

Thirty years on, Baqer Moin said, in his interview with the Radio 4 Document programme, that like many other Iranians he was not pro-Shah, but more in favour of the rule of law and human rights and against censorship. 'I wasn't in favor of the Shah but I never campaigned in any sense,' says Moin. 'The BBC was really very careful not to have anybody active in politics to be participating in the programmes of the Persian Service.' However, when pressed, he said he was 'pro-revolution like many others in the country'.[94] There were also examples given by BBC staff that suggested an opposite dynamic to that described by Brown. Lutfali Khonji recalls how once at the height of tension between the Shah and the FCO, the BBC's head of the Eastern Service, Mark Dodd, blocked his interview with Ayatollah Khomeini:

> At the time interviewing was done with great technical difficulty. We had to book studios and lines. I also had to speak to several

contacts before convincing them of the justifications for the interview. Nevertheless, soon after arriving in the studio, Mark Dodd, the head of BBC World Service, arrived in the studio. I don't even know who had informed him that I was doing this interview. He barred me from interviewing and said we should not artificially blow the events out of proportion.[95]

Khonji uses this example to refute the common belief that the BBC was supporting the Islamic revolution in Iran. He says if that were the case they would not be blocking an interview with Khomeini. In 2010, at a witness seminar on the role of the BBC in the Iranian Revolution of 1979, there was wry amusement from Dodd and others at the BBC refusing the first televised interview with Khomeini since he wasn't 'important enough'.[96] This decision was again interpreted as evidence of autonomous decision making and the absence of political privileging in Persian Service coverage of events.

However, the documents of the Foreign Office indicate that pressure had been put on the British government from Iran to stop Khomeini's statements being read out on the BBC because invariably in his interviews he called for the downfall of the Shah. Khonji recalls that after about three weeks Mark Dodd did allow an interview with Khomeini, but two BBC staff went to Paris later to conduct the interview; one was Iranian and the other British. This famous interview with Ayatollah Khomeini came under strong scrutiny later for failing to meet journalistic standards.

The FCO was alarmed when Mark Dodd informed them about the plan to interview Khomeini. At the foreign policy meeting on 30 October 1978, serious concern was expressed. The minutes of the meeting record that 'this was a development of such potential seriousness' that the FCO was 'justified in taking the matter up with the BBC at a high level'.[97] John Leahy, the Assistant Under-Secretary for information services at the FCO who had written the minutes of the meeting, says he told the meeting that he hoped 'the BBC were not contemplating interviewing Khomeini'. He stressed 'we have already gone as far as we should'. Leahy, who had served as Head of Chancery in the Tehran embassy, looked after relations with Bush House. The main issue was how to stop the BBC from broadcasting an interview with Khomeini. The directive from the Foreign Secretary, David Owen, was that the BBC should not be approached directly. He had repeatedly emphasized the importance of the BBC's independence in his correspondence. This was, however, always coupled with a word of caution that left room for making protests to the BBC. For example, in his letter to Sir Michael Swann, the BBC's Chairman of the Board of Governors, on 14 December 1978, following the complaints, Owen said:

> I am a strong believer in the independence of the BBC and the value of the BBC's external broadcasts. I have therefore been scrupulous about defending your independence at all stages. I believe it would be gravely damaging to the long-term future of Britain's standing in the world if there were to be an attempt of Government interference. I have, however, to assure myself that you and your board are fully aware of the criticisms from foreign governments and I feel it is my responsibility to satisfy myself that you have given the representations of foreign governments full consideration.[98]

Owen accepted that FCO financing of the external services presented a problem, but reiterated that he would tell the Iranian Foreign Minister in their meeting about the BBC's 'editorial independence'.[99] However, Leahy revealed in his minutes of the 30 October meeting that there had been an 'agreement' of some sort with the BBC, which could have been a reference to the Licence and Agreement of 1969: 'In terms of the agreement we have with them [the BBC] they are obliged to obtain and accept such information regarding conditions in and the policies of HM Government [...] as will enable the Corporation to plan and prepare its programmes in the external services in the national interest.'[100] Leahy doubted that the BBC would forego the interview with Khomeini and indeed, if they did, there was a risk that this would become known and then the FCO would be seen to be putting pressure on the BBC. A few days later, on

9 November 1978, the news of the Persian Service interview was confirmed. Foreign Secretary Owen wrote to the embassy in Tehran: 'I'm afraid I took [Mark] Dodd's last assurance to mean that they were not going through with the proposed interview with Khomeini for the Persian Service.'[101] So despite their attempts, the FCO had not managed to stop the broadcast. Foreign Secretary Owen was informed that he had tried too late and although he had delayed it, he had not managed to stop the interview. But he stated that the main concern had been that there might have been a call to arms in the interview, but no such calls were expressed in the interview:

> I telephoned Mark Dodd who made enquiries and came back to say the BBC could find no such phrase in any of the broadcasts quoting Khomeini. He added that the Persian Service is not carrying any statements by Khomeini.[102]

The Persian Service had contacted a close aid to Khomeini, Abolhasan Banisadr (later president of Iran), and asked him to help set up an interview with Khomeini. The Ayatollah had rejected the idea, but Banisadr persuaded him to change his mind: 'I convinced him when I said all the other media you give interviews to are also foreign so what is the difference!' Khomeini then accepted.[103] He asked that questions be faxed to him in Paris and this was done, although David Perman of the World Service, who accompanied Ferydoon Jahed to conduct the interview, did not know about this. Perman says that at the time this was not so important:

> We know it is an important interview now, with hindsight. At the time most of us did not even know what an Ayatollah was, we could not even imagine he would one day be the leader of Iran. We wanted democracy for Iran. We went to this village outside Paris, went to his room and sat down cross-legged. He would have no eye contact with us. Areas of questioning were agreed with the Ayatollah. When I asked a question about the minorities, he answered it but then turned back to his aides who told us if there

were any other unwritten question, he would stop the interview immediately. I did not know there were written questions.[104]

In the March 2009 radio documentary on this subject, Perman said the result was that 'the Ayatollah did use it as a platform for his views', but it 'was surprising and [...] it was not our intention to give him such a platform [...] to that extent it was not a good interview, I wasn't able to press him with supplementary questions'. On the other hand, he thinks it was still 'a good interview because it did show what we were facing'.[105] Looking back, Mark Dodd, then head of the Eastern Service and responsible for the content, thinks this was an 'unsatisfactory' basis for conducting an interview, but sees much journalistic value in getting the interview from a man who 'himself was the story':

> What we could get out of him was going to illuminate the character of the man. You could make a case for the interview but I think it was flawed. Our coverage was not as full as we would have wished, there were mistakes, there were gaps, I am not for a moment saying this was an impeccable Service. There were occasions when we made mistakes, I am still sorry that we made those mistakes but they were infinitely less than our critics suggested.[106]

The FCO began monitoring the Persian Service in December 1978, just two months before the revolution. The Research Department wrote back to the Embassy in Tehran saying that none of the broadcasts they heard indicated any 'false inflections', there were no 'obvious' examples of 'slanting or distortion' and the overall content and presentation of material also seemed 'quite well balanced'. They reported that there was, however, some evidence of looseness of editorial supervision and 'words were often translated in three or four different ways', but none of the words could be said to have been 'stronger' in tone than the others.[107] In the letter analysing the overall results of monitoring the Persian broadcasts, Chris Rundle of the Research Department stated that perhaps inevitably, with the opposition activities in the last few weeks, 'there has been more time spent on reporting opposition than government activities' and that much of the reporting would 'not have been to the liking of the Iranian authorities'.[108] On 11 December, the BBC's reporting of the demonstrations on the religious day of Ashura was picked as one of the samples of broadcast. The report speaks of a 17-article resolution that is 'due to be announced' by the opposition.[109] It claims that the main point of the opposition resolution is to assert 'complete support for Ayatollah Khomeini' who has been 'the most serious and outspoken person in his idea for the overthrow of the Shah':

> Large crowds of people have again gathered in Tehran and other cities in Iran to take part in religious ceremonies and also in demonstrations against the Shah. It is estimated that the size of the crowd going to Shahyad Square was even greater than the one million who were there yesterday. Our reporter says that the demonstrators were more militant than yesterday and the slogans were not only religious but made explicit attacks on the Shah himself and the Crown Prince and many of them called for his death. The BBC correspondent in Tehran said that for kilometers nothing could be seen but banners and flags [...] the religious leaders read aloud a declaration in support of their leader Ayatollah Khomeini who is living in Paris.[110]

Was this truly a departure from BBC Persian Service's style of reporting in the previous years or was it a reflection of the breadth and depth of events happening in Iran? The large-scale demonstrations on the two holy days of the Shi'a calendar, Tasua and Ashura, were impressive and they were reported in detail by almost all the international press. The *New York Times* reported that the two days had shown that the government was powerless to preserve law and order on its own, while the *Washington Post* hailed it as 'adding considerable weight to the opposition's claim of being an alternative government'. Similarly, the *Christian Science Monitor* reported that 'a giant wave of humanity swept through the capital declaring louder than any bullet or bomb could the clear message that "The Shah must go".[111] So the BBC

Persian Service was not alone in reporting the significance of the day. As it was staffed by Persian nationals, the likelihood increases of detailed and at times somewhat partial reporting. However, the BBC could not be seen to have been creating or pre-empting the events. Indeed, another example was sent of the broadcast on 14 December of pro-Shah demonstrators:

> In Iran demonstrations in support of the Shah have taken place. The biggest of them is in Isfahan. But Western correspondents who were flown to Isfahan say that it is strongly suspected that the demonstrations were to some extent arranged specially for them. One of the BBC correspondents says that many of the 30,000 people who took part in the demonstrations had obviously come to Isfahan from the surrounding villages, or been brought here from there. According to Radio Iran, which is under government control, other demonstrations in support of the government took place in several other towns including Tehran.[112]

The broader question of the impartiality of reporters at major historical conjunctures could be debated in relation to reporting during the weeks and months leading to the Iranian Revolution. It is often the journalists themselves who carry the general tone of the news. At the time, the recruitment criteria in the BBC English World Service and in the language services were different: BBC English reporters were recruited after several tests on their reporting skills, while those in language services were recruited mainly for their translation skills. They were not recruited as producers at that stage and were referred to as programme assistants and translators. Consequently, programme assistants did not have any control over content and could not, or should not, have editorialized. However, under the circumstances and given the speed of incoming news and developments, these roles must have been confusing. Editorial scrutiny may have been challenging and individual staff preferences could have contributed to the tone and selection of news items. That is perhaps why there were complaints that 'the BBC has been infiltrated by anti-Shah elements', a claim strongly refuted by the BBC who had time and again to explain that BBC Persian recording was done by translating English dispatches written by BBC correspondents in Iran.[113]

Asked in a recent interview about the opinion of staff at the time, Khonji believes that 'it was a true reflection of Iranian society at home and abroad'.[114] He said about 80 per cent of the staff supported the revolution and only 20 per cent opposed it and that the reason for the increased popularity of the BBC could have been the better communication with the opposition, as well as the fact that Radio Iran was on strike. In addition, the nightly electricity blackouts produced by striking workers also shut down NIRT's television news broadcasts; however, BBC radio could be listened to on shortwave with battery-operated radios.[115] BBC Persian Service staff also believed that the BBC itself had become far more open to newer methods of production. Khonji and other members of staff interviewed all strongly rejected the assertion that the British government was pro-revolution or used the BBC to further that aim. They say there was never any pressure on any member of the staff during the months leading up to the revolution.[116] During the final three months, the Iranian Embassy's press attaché, Mehrdad Khonsary, was tasked with listening to the BBC Persian broadcasts on a daily basis. He was to check the English reports filed by the BBC journalists in Tehran against what was reported from the Persian Service. He told the witness seminar at SOAS in March 2010 that he could not 'find any mistakes in the translation'. However, he said that 'the nuances were worked in the broadcasts through the stresses and punctuations' on certain words in such a way that made the meaning different in Persian.[117]

On 1 December 1978, Radji wrote to the British Foreign Secretary to inform him that the BBC representative had been summoned to the Ministry to explain his misrepresentation of facts and that 'his expulsion seemed probable'.[118] Andrew Whitley was subsequently expelled from Iran; 30 years on Whitley says he was not surprised at the anger of the Shah and his supporters. The BBC Persian broadcasts had 'a huge impact, everyone heard the programme, everyone I spoke to anywhere in Tehran and other major cities, listened to the BBC. Whitley states that he was pro-revolution: 'they had justice on their side [...] I personally believed that change was overdue in Iran [...] However, I was not in any way advocating either for a leftist revolution or for the overthrow of the Shah.'[119]

So did the BBC fan the flames of revolution? Whitley said he 'would not use those words but the BBC did play a role [...] If it was not for the BBC's broadcasts into the country and its huge listenership I think that the revolution would not have proceeded as quickly as it did [...] The BBC ought to be careful about over-stepping the line between reporting and being seen as part and parcel of the opposition movement. I don't believe the BBC – as a foreign broadcasting organization – ought to be in a position of attempting to change domestic events but I wouldn't put intent on our side,' Whitley concluded.[120] However, political developments were so interesting that the world media were reporting on events and the BBC was no exception. Yet the BBC Persian Service remained the lead broadcaster in Iran and for Iranians around the world. It covered the smallest details of a set of political developments that had taken the world by storm. It enjoyed direct contacts with the leaders of the political movement to topple the Shah and it would have been professional suicide not to use these opportunities. Iranian supporters of the revolution regarded the BBC with great warmth and considered it to be a trustable medium for the information they needed to get about political developments inside Iran.

However, to report only on the opposition to the Shah may have been to forego the BBC's claim to objectivity and balance in reporting. Unsurprisingly, Iranian supporters of the Shah continued to view the BBC's role most sceptically. Ambassador Radji's accounts of meetings in London reveal that anger with the BBC was persistent and threatened to get out of hand.[121] According to his account, various members of the Iranian government who wanted to express complaints to the BBC were told that the BBC acted independently.[122] Some influential Iranians also decided to put pressure on the BBC's Persian Service through complaints to the FCO and the BBC Board of Governors. FCO documents reveal the protestations made by several figures such as Seyyed Hossein Nasr, head of Queen Farah's office, and the Iranian millionaire, David Alliance. They argued that the Persian Service 'does not adhere to the British standards of fair play' and tabled a five-page detailed breakdown of his criticism of BBC broadcasts.[123] Nasr made a direct complaint to the FCO that even those Iranians who were not anti-BBC 'resented its interference in Iran's affairs'. He claimed that there was 'a general belief that the Persian Service was acting in furtherance of a joint British–Soviet plan to undermine the American position' and that the gesture from David Owen was only 'part of the act'.[124] Parsons wrote from Tehran that 'for historical reasons we are credited here with more political influence than is commensurate with our power. What we do or say is, therefore, of disproportionate significance [...] I therefore believe that it is right for us to continue to support the Shah and his government both in private and in public'.[125] In an account of his own perception of events, the Shah accuses the mass media of playing an important role in the unfolding of events in Iran during the three years leading up to the revolution. He said the composition of journalists in search of 'ever more sensational news led to the most regrettable excesses'.[126] The Shah went on to blame the BBC:

> No less surprising was the BBC's attitude. From the beginning of 1978 their Persian language broadcasts consisted of virulent attacks against my regime. It was as though some mysterious conductor had given the go ahead to these attacks. I am not mentioning the attitude of certain special envoys that caused certain deplorable incidents to be magnified out of all proportion. I am tempted to say that, for some newspapers a dead body is a godsend and I think that some newsagents must have made a fortune out of the events in Iran.[127]

Whatever the Shah and his supporters might have assumed, there does not seem to have been any intention on the part of the British government to destabilize the Shah. Foreign Office documents show clearly that the British government saw in the

Shah the most suitable leader for guarding British interests. It was only in September 1978 – five months before the revolution in Iran – that the British government recognized the first signs of the possible downfall of the Shah and the FCO and Downing Street were both 'shocked' at the prospect.[128] The Middle East Department at the FCO began to assess possible scenarios and still came to the conclusion that 'in the present climate of uncertainty prevailing in the region from Afghanistan to the Horn of Africa, the Shah is a vital bastion against Soviet encroachment with enormous threats which that presents to Western oil supplies and to our trade'.[129] Lucas of the FCO Middle East Department wrote to the Prime Minister: 'The Shah represents the best prospect for orderly progress in Iran itself. He is a hyper sensitive man with long memory (which broods upon the British role in deposing his father). Any wavering in the support of his friends and allies [UK and US] will accordingly have adverse effects on him.'[130] The Foreign Office also suggested that if any regime from the opposition groups active in Iran were to succeed the Shah, 'ranging from communist dominated revolutionary regime to reactionary Muslim system', Iran would become 'hostile to Western interests, as well as probably failing to assert control over the country'.[131]

Thus, the British government did not in any way welcome the perceived alternative political scenarios. When Ayatollah Khomeini was forced to leave Iraq, the British Foreign Secretary, David Owen, wrote in a confidential telegram advising 'the farther away from Iran he [Khomeini] is, the better', adding that Iranians may rest assured that 'we should have no official contacts with Khomeini'.[132] In September 1978, the then British Prime Minister, James Callaghan, wrote an actual letter of support to the Shah, in which he noted that it was sad that 'all this should happen at a time when your Imperial Majesty's leadership has been moving steadily in the direction of becoming a modern industrial society'.[133]

Nor indeed was the US supporting anyone other than the Shah until as late as January 1979. The deputy Secretary of State, Warren Christopher, was quoted in FCO meetings as saying that the US was looking to give 'psychological and other support' to the Shah, whom they regarded as 'the only vehicle of stability in the country.'[134] In Anglo–American planning talks in Washington on 10 October 1978, Henry Precht, the US Country Director for Iran, defined the events in Iran as 'the worst foreign policy disaster that had hit the West.'[135] He went on to describe the situation in cataclysmic terms, but while recognizing 'essentially that the whole population is against the Shah and wanted his removal', he nevertheless believed that 'the current policy of UK and US to support the Shah was the right one' and that there would be 'nothing to be gained' by a change of policy. This was despite the fact that Precht held 'very small hopes of survival for the Shah'. Given Precht's position in the US State Department, the British authorities attending the planning talks found his words 'significant'.[136] Likewise, George Griffin, a US intelligence analyst, said in a meeting on 7 December 1978 with his British counterparts that 'we know the Shah is a manic depressive: we don't think he is capable of coping without some kind of American guidance', but nevertheless he too believed that 'the US should work actively to create a civilian coalition under the Shah's leadership'. Griffin argued that if the Shah stepped down there was a good chance of 'the army losing control of the country and turning on itself'.[137]

In the final two months prior to the revolution, political developments were unfolding so fast that they surprised the international community. The British and the Americans, who since the Anglo–American coup of 1953 which returned the Shah to power had been at the forefront of political decision making, were now at a loss about what to do with the Shah. The movement for the removal of the Shah was gaining strength beyond their control. The escalating strikes in the oilfields, on the Iranian airline service, at electrical power plants and other key sectors of Iran's industry were crippling the economy. Acute shortages of fuel, gasoline and other vital commodities were causing riots and demonstrations, indicating that the Shah was increasingly losing power. The prospects for the military government of General Azhari seemed to be growing dim. Western leaders were finding it hard to predict whether the Shah could survive the storm and remain as powerful as he had been over the past decade. Ambassador Sullivan gives a clear account of the confusion within the US administration[138] between various policy makers including President Carter, the US Secretary of State Cyrus Vance and the Iran policy chief Zbigniew Brzezinski, as to whether to use a harsher military option to save the Shah or to forego his chances. They did not know how to equate such military action with their overt demands for improved human rights in Iran. Sullivan claims that he was awaiting instruction from President Carter for over two months but this was not forthcoming. He also says that the Shah wanted to know what the US thought of his taking a tougher military stance. It was on 9 November 1978 that Sullivan had written his report 'Thinking the Unthinkable' about having to consider a replacement for the Shah if the military government of General Azhari failed to restore order.[139] He explains how, after months of waiting for an answer to his report, 'the United States government was facing the situation in Iran with no policy whatsoever'.[140] But it was only on 5 January 1979 that the US President, Jimmy Carter, changed his position of backing the Shah. 'It now suddenly became clear to him [the Shah], as it had to me,' says Sullivan, 'that we [the US] had no design whatsoever and that our government's actions were being guided by some inexplicable whim.'[141]

The change in the position of the US and other international players could relate to the Shah's illness, which had been known about since August 1978 but was only perceived as acute, especially by the French, toward the end of the year.[142] The French president, Giscard d'Estaing, sent his personal representative, Michel Poniatowski, to Iran on 27–28 December 1978. He subsequently reported that 'the Shah was sick, suffering from a cancer that was relatively under control but strongly affecting his well-being'.[143] The Shah had finally organized the actions that were necessary for a constitutional investiture of the nationalist politician Shapour Bakhtiar. A regency council had been appointed and all was in preparation for the government transition. 'About this time,' says Sullivan, 'I received a message asking me to see the Shah and inform him that the United States government felt it was in his best interest and in Iran's for him to leave the country.'[144] The Shah left Iran on 16 January and Ayatollah Khomeini arrived on 2 February. Sullivan was in fact so angered by this lack of clarity in the US policy that he tendered his resignation and refused to accept other diplomatic posts because he did not 'have confidence in the judgment of the president in times of crisis.'[145] As far as the British government was concerned the 'massive demonstrations' of December had shown 'the extent of genuine opposition to the Shah'. The line to take for the cabinet and the press issued on 14 December 1978 stated that 'the support which the demonstrators apparently gave to Khomeini indicated that it will now be indeed very difficult for a constitutional solution to the crisis to be found under which a broad-based civilian administration would be prepared to govern in the Shah's name as a purely constitutional monarch'. The conclusion for the British position was:

> There is little we can do to influence the situation. The Iranians must work out their own salvation. But they may soon face a position in which even the alternatives to the present regime can be no more damaging, particularly from the economic point of view.[146]

Barely one month after the Iranian Revolution, on 2 March 1979, the late columnist Christopher Hitchens wrote a damning attack on British attempts at trying to influence the BBC. Under the heading 'How They Tried to Bend the BBC', Hitchens categorized those who complained about BBC Persian Service's broadcasts as either 'right-wing sages like Julian Amery, Lord Chalfont, Woodrow Wyatt, Lord George Brown' and others who 'maintained a barrage of semi-public calumny against the BBC's coverage of Iran', or those in the Foreign Office who wanted to control the Persian Service's broadcasts: 'In one case the Foreign Office were able to reach a senior BBC official at home and give him an advance Persian Government view that the interview with Khomeini was inflammatory.' Hitchens criticized British officials for even wanting to control the BBC:

The Shah and his minions can hardly be blamed for trying to protect their crumbling regime. It is, however, another thing for the British Government to try to help them by attacking the independence of British journalism. On a number of occasions in the past the BBC has modified or postponed broadcasts to accommodate desires in Whitehall.[147]

We have seen in this chapter how the memory of the role of the British government and the BBC during Reza Shah's forced abdication in 1941 and the Anglo–American coup of 1953 had tarnished the British image in Iran. The Shah, who had incidentally benefited from both episodes, could not believe that the British were supporting him. He blamed the BBC Persian broadcasts as proof of that misplaced belief. The reality was that BBC Persian broadcasts took the lead in reporting the Iranian Revolution of 1979 and both the BBC management and the FCO were taken by surprise. The FCO was caught in the middle. On the one hand, an important element of British foreign policy was being played out: the BBC was communicating closely with Iranians. On the other hand, the Shah, an important British ally in the Middle East, a trusted friend and a wealthy political/military partner, was angered and devastated by the broadcasts.

At the same time, these were trying times for the BBC Persian Service, which was coming out of its indifferent mould of the 1960s when reports were simply written by British journalists, and translated by Iranian staff recruited not as producers but translators. The Service was taking a leap into professional journalism, contacting the opposition and broadcasting their views. BBC Persian Service radio has probably never been as popular as it was in the year leading up to the revolution. Yet it has also never been seen to be as partial in its news reporting as it was during those years, at times even seen to be overstepping the line. The collective memory of these early days came to haunt the British government again in January 2009 when BBC PTV was set up, as we will see in Chapter 6.

5

BBC Broadcasting to Afghanistan

Historically, the majority of the population in Afghanistan have listened to the BBC's Persian Service since Persian – known as Dari in Afghanistan and spoken predominantly by the Tajik ethnic group – has always been one of the two main official languages of the country. Moreover, for much of Afghan history, Persian was considered to be the official language spoken by most of the six ethnic groups forming the mosaic of Afghanistan's population.

However, significant pockets of the population in the influential southern Pashtun provinces had long approached the BBC and the British government for broadcasts in the Pashto language. Estimates vary but Pashtuns in Afghanistan form about 42 per cent of the population, estimated to be around 25 million. They also form some 13 per cent of the population of Pakistan and many live in India and Iran.[1] They have always played a significant role in the politics of both Afghanistan and Pakistan although they suffer from chronic inter-tribal feuds. For over a decade, broadcasts in the Pashto language were seen as an unnecessary addition by the FCO, which funds the language services of the BBC. Since the BBC already broadcast in Persian and Urdu, the view in the FCO traditionally was that there was no need for an additional Pashto service, but as Afghanistan became a crisis point in East–West relations, that position changed dramatically. The Soviet invasion of Afghanistan during the 1980s provided potent political reasons for establishing the Pashto Service, while the civil war of the 1990s that culminated in the rule of the Pashto-speaking Taliban, and the 9/11 attack and the subsequent war in Afghanistan, have provided ample rationale for its maintenance.

Pashto broadcasts began on 15 August 1981 and the combined broadcasts in Persian and Pashto meant that an overwhelming majority of the population in Afghanistan listened to the BBC. In periods of crisis, war or political change, BBC popularity would suddenly rise to staggering figures. During the years of civil war in the 1990s, for instance, and especially after Taliban rule began in 1996, BBC statistics show that almost 90 per cent of the adult population listened. Moreover, the BBC Persian and Pashto broadcasts had a large, loyal audience among the 6 million Afghan refugees living in Pakistan, Iran and the Persian Gulf states.[2] Even by 2003 the BBC, in its Annual Review, still claimed 82 per cent weekly audiences in Kabul:

> BBC World Service is the leading broadcaster in Kabul with an unprecedented 82 per cent of adults in the capital listening to BBC broadcasts in Persian and Pashto every week.[3]

In 2013, the BBC still claims some 60 per cent weekly listenership, but despite closer political ties between the UK and Afghanistan and despite the fact that the BBC has several powerful FM stations across the country, the percentage of listeners has dropped, mainly due to the multiplicity of local media now available.

As was the case with Iran, Persian and Pashto broadcasts of the BBC become a potent tool for political communication at three important political conjunctures in Afghanistan: namely the Soviet invasion of Afghanistan in 1980; the early 1990s when the Western-backed Mujahedin came to power and civil war ensued both amongst the Mujahedin and with the Taliban; and post 9/11 when the US-led international forces ousted the Taliban and a new chapter was opened in Western relations with Afghanistan.

Changing priorities of the FCO

Pashto was not considered one of the necessary language sections to be included in the big BBC World Service expansion of the 1940s by the Foreign Office. The main focus at the time of war was to counteract German war propaganda. While Sir Reader Bullard, the British minister in Iran, had drawn attention to the large number of Germans in Iranian territory that had been invited in by the Iranian government, in Afghanistan the number of Germans was seen to be much smaller.[4]

Despite repeated requests from Afghanistan for transmission in the Pashto language, this was rejected by the Foreign Office. Even the first documented suggestion – made by Mr Roshan, the Afghan deputy minister of information – is for including Dari speakers from Afghanistan in the Persian broadcasts. Then the FCO, interested in the potential expansion of BBC listenership in the region, wrote to the Director of External Broadcasting, Oliver Whitley, in February 1969:

> Mr Roshan claims that those who speak the sort of Persian used at the moment on the Persian Service numbered no more than 15 million, whereas those who would be happier with the sort of Persian spoken in Afghanistan were perhaps 40 million. Although of course he may be assumed to be overstating the case, we are, nevertheless, very interested in his contention that the injection of Afghan Persian into the service would bring dividends outside the territory of Afghanistan, particularly in the USSR. [This is a reference to Tajikistan, an independent republic since 1991, where the language is also Persian.][5]

The BBC was also keen to have more Persian-speaking audiences but disputed Roshan's figures. 'Dari could reach some seven million in Afghanistan,' the Head of the Eastern Service, Mark Dodd, wrote in a letter to Charles Thompson of the Guidance and Information Policy Department at the FCO, 'and we understand some further two million or so Tajiks in the USSR,' but there was no evidence of 'a potential mass audience for Dari'. Dodd further argued that in mixing the style of Persian 'there could be a danger of reducing our effectiveness to Iran'; the Persian Service was 'prescribed to serve Iran' and that if they tried to 'blend the transmission' to be suited to both countries then the BBC could 'fall between two stools'. He brushed off complaints that 'traditionalist elements' in Afghanistan might find some of the programmes offensive by saying that listeners' letters and field surveys had shown 'young people are among our most ardent listeners' and that our service is 'Iranian orientated'.[6]

In a separate note Dodd seemed to suggest that a 'Pashto transmission from London would have potentially the wider audience and its spill over in Pakistan [...] could bring in a potential audience of around 13 million'. He argued that in Afghanistan Pashto is the language of 'the people and the aristocracy' while Dari is the language of the upper middle classes, who are 'of course an important target'. He says that those who want to listen in Dari have the opportunity to hear the Persian news and current affairs, but the Pashto speakers have 'no such opportunity'. He concludes that a brief separate transmission for Afghanistan in Pashto would be 'well worth considering'.[7]

Eight months later, in December 1971, the State visit of the Afghan King, Zahir Shah, provided the chance for a one-off test of what later became known as the 'Kabul tapes'. These were recorded in London and made especially for Afghanistan. The then Head of the Persian Service, John Dunn, reported to Dodd on 14 December about how well the recorded programmes had gone. 'During the period 2–13 December daily documentary features were broadcast giving background information on Britain and British institutions,' he wrote. These included features on the British monarchy, the British parliamentary system, the Guildhall and the government of London and Buckingham and St James's Palaces.[8]

Six months later, in a report to Dodd, Dunn makes a fresh proposal. He suggests rescheduling the Persian *Dawn* transmission and getting extra time from the African broadcasts that ran before the Persian broadcasts in order to create a special slot 'for a Dari and Pashto magazine'. Another possibility was to have a midday transmission aimed primarily at audiences in Afghanistan, but 'to have greater impact in Afghanistan', Dunn concluded, 'we should also mount a live news transmission, preferably in Pashto at 0900'.[9] He suggested that these programmes would only be transmitted in shortwave and that the cost was relatively low for the FCO.

Dunn argued that 'all ministers and officials in Afghanistan are known to listen to the BBC Persian Service' and there was 'clearly considerable listening among the people of influence'. Letters from listeners were included with the report to encourage the FCO. But despite all Dunn's efforts, the FCO showed little interest in funding a Pashto service. Partly, it claimed to have evidence that the Persian Service was adequate.

In July 1973, after 40 years of monarchy, Zahir Shah was toppled while on a trip to Italy and his cousin, Mohammed Daud, seized power in a coup. Daud declared a republic and tried to pit the Soviets off against Western powers. But his style alienated left-wing factions who joined forces against him, and he also alienated Pakistan in disagreements over the 'Pakhtunistan' question.[10]

And still the FCO felt there was no need for a separate service, since existing broadcasts were providing a good service, even informing Afghans about the coup. An Afghan specialist writes to the FCO:

> In Afghanistan I heard the BBC whilst I was living with a tribe of nomads, the Quchis. They lived in the remote Central and Eastern areas of Afghanistan. Their chief, a Khan of some importance in the area, used to listen regularly to the BBC Farsi broadcasts. He was extremely well informed and pro-British. The BBC had been his first informant about the 1973 coup.[11]

Although it was not possible to conduct sample surveys about audiences in Afghanistan, a confidential report by the Foreign Office claimed there was widespread listening in Afghanistan. In July 1974 the British Embassy Information Policy Report on Afghanistan concluded:

The greatest impact made by the British information effort is that of the BBC. The Persian Service is widely listened to. If the BBC succeeds in introducing even a short service in Dari, the audiences may be further increased. BBC news bulletins are also regularly monitored and used by Radio Afghanistan.[12]

A Foreign Office report suggested that the Persian Service 'is understood by Dari speaking Afghans' and, since there was no additional expense involved in transmitting this service to Afghanistan as well as Iran, that should suffice.[13] It was argued that despite its 'Teheran accent' the Persian Service attracted 'substantial audience', including the 'educated Afghan elite both in Kabul and other parts of Afghanistan'. Moreover, the attitude of the Service towards Afghanistan is 'favourable' and thus it serves the 'national interests'. Complaints were not seen to be important enough since 'BBC objectivity more than compensates for any occasional slight differences between the editorial attitudes of the BBC and the policy of HMG'. The main criticism that an audience survey would reveal was that the Persian Service included 'too few items specifically related to Afghanistan'.[14]

Thus the idea of a separate Pashto Service did not receive attention until Radio Iran introduced one hour of Pashto transmission on 7 May 1974. The BBC Eastern Service then put in a bid to the Foreign Office for a Dari/Pashto service based on recruiting six programme assistants, arguing that it must be able to compete. But even a reduced version, recruiting only three programme assistants, was rejected.

Finally, Mark Dodd, the head of the BBC Eastern Service, decided to go for the cheapest option of replacing a ten-minute music slot at the end of Persian broadcasts with Dari news. Writing to the Persian Programme Organizer on 27 August 1974, he revealed that the Foreign Office still refused to pay and that the money – which had been put aside for Dari tapes for Kabul – would be used instead for Dari broadcasts.[15]

The flurry of activity between 1970 and 1979 that included numerous meetings, surveys, discussions and exchange of letters revealed FCO funding to be the key issue. But neither the professional opinions of the programme makers, nor demands from inside countries for broadcasts in a specific language, seem to matter enough to convince the FCO to make funds available.

In the end, it was Afghanistan's changing political fortunes that altered the FCO view. In 1978 the pro-communist Democratic Party overthrew Mohammed Daud in a coup. Two separate leftist leaders, Hafizulah Amin and Normohamad Taraki, from rival factions of the Party, fought for power, but eventually in 1980 a third member of the same party, Babrak Karmal, backed by Soviet troops, was installed as leader. Heavy fighting ensued until the Soviet invasion of Afghanistan.

Setting up the Pashto Service: 1981–3

The Soviet invasion of Afghanistan happened soon after the Islamic Revolution of 1979 in Iran when the Persian Service was deeply involved in reporting on Iran. So Dodd asked David Page, the head of the Urdu Service of the BBC, to set up a Pashto Service; 30 years on, Page says that he firmly believes that it was the Soviet invasion of Afghanistan that finally 'persuaded the Foreign Office to begin Pashto language broadcasts to communicate with the people of Afghanistan'. However, he stresses that there was never any suggestion of editorial interference.[16]

The first task, according to Page, was to find out what the most suitable Pashto accent would be. The BBC was not allowed inside Afghanistan during the years of Soviet occupation and this explains why all research and recruitment was initially done from Pakistan. Being the head of the Urdu Service, Page naturally had better contacts inside Pakistan and most of his advisors were Pakistanis, so most of the news-gathering was done from Pakistan. Previously, news about Afghanistan was only available from the BBC correspondent in either Islamabad or Delhi. In fact, it was Mark Tully, the BBC's correspondent in India, who had reported the 1978 coup against General Daud. After the

Soviet invasion, not only Afghanistan but also Pakistan, as the other front-line state, became globally far more important.[17]

Pakistan was also the home of most of the Mujahedin groups that fought the pro-communist governments in Kabul. Pakistan's government, and its military intelligence service, the Inter-Services Intelligence (ISI), as well as Pakistan's influential Pashtun tribes, became even more active than before in trying to influence the politics of Afghanistan. With the exception of Ahmad Shah Massoud and Ismail Khan, all the Mujahedin leaders were based in the North-West Frontier Province of Pakistan bordering the federally administered tribal areas of Wazirestan. The fight against communism was being organized from this area and often led by the ISI and the CIA.

In 1983, Page travelled to Peshawar and interviewed all six Mujahedin heads. Asked if this had been initiated by the FCO, Page said: 'Absolutely not [...] It was my very own idea as a journalist and I just wanted to understand these people better.' During 1981–3 the Pashto Section became increasingly important in the eyes of the FCO but it didn't interfere in programme content. 'The head of Eastern Service, Mark Dodd, was not keen for us to be too close to the Foreign Office. He wanted the BBC to remain independent,' says Page.[18]

BBC Pashto broadcasts were initially for 15 minutes a day. The World Service newsroom remained the main provider of all items that were translated from English into Pashto for broadcasts. By the time Page left the Pashto Section in 1985 the programmes had been extended to 30 minutes a day, although the BBC was still not allowed to send reporters inside Afghanistan.

The second stage: 1983–94

In 1983, Gordon Adam became the Head of the Pashto Service. Adam, who was originally an analyst in the Eastern Topical Unit of the BBC World Service, recalls that as a reporter he was desperate to get accurate information from inside Afghanistan.

Finally, a senior member of the Foreign Office 'agreed to send me FCO's Situation Reports from Kabul' and he also managed to get transcriptions of the US Embassy weekly press conferences in Islamabad. This seemed a practical way of creating a balance between what was reported from inside Afghanistan and Pakistan. So much of the reporting was linked to diplomatic cables.

Adam says that FCO officials were 'very keen on the BBC covering the war in Afghanistan and they were keen for us to cover stories about the Mujahedin standing up to the Soviets'. He believes that the UK 'was generally following US policy on the war in Afghanistan' and they wanted the Mujahedin to be portrayed well since 'the US was using the Afghan anger against the Soviets for its own political motives'.[19] Finally, in 1987, Adam, together with George Arney of the BBC World Service and a *Guardian* reporter, managed to get permission to report from inside Afghanistan and, in 1988, Adam managed to employ the first local 'stringer' to report for the BBC from Peshawar:

> Our new reporter on Afghanistan, Hamed Elmi, became a fantastic source of news and operations for all BBC activity. And this basic initiative was slowly built up as an infrastructure for getting news and information from Kabul and Islamabad. We then managed to have the Afghan President's approval for Lyse Doucet to be BBC resident correspondent in Kabul. She stayed during 1987–88 and it meant our reporting from the capital was transformed.[20]

Lyse Doucet's placement in Kabul became possible through another diplomatic contact; the intervention of President Najibullah's brother-in-law, Ahmad Sarvar, posted to London as *chargé d'affaires* of Afghanistan, 'helped us to get to Afghanistan'.[21]

Pashto broadcasts soon developed a huge following. Now not only was there reporting from a journalist based in Kabul but there were direct interviews with warring factions. 'Even the 15-minute programme had 82 per cent listenership in Afghanistan,' says Gordon Adam. In 1988 more than '50,000 letters were received from listeners' and the BBC became an important part of people's life. This, according to Adam, was testimony to the careful use of language taking into consideration the delicate differences between the differing Pashto accents in Pakistan and Afghanistan.

From 1986 the relationship between the BBC and the FCO changed. Prior to that, the BBC 'was at the beck and call of the FCO' as far as choice of languages was concerned, but 'this did not include content'. However, according to Adam, 'later the BBC could propose languages and duration for FCO approval'.[22] In fact, the preferred style by which the FCO managed the BBC changed so that the BBC directors were given specific budgets and heads of services and regions took on more responsibility for the way they spent budgets. At the end of the year they had to meet their own set targets.

In 1989 when John Tusa became the Director-General of the BBC World Service, he transformed BBC World Service's journalistic standards and methods. He was keen to modernize the style of journalism in the various language services and wanted more direct interviewing mixed with reports prepared by Central Talks and Features Department. He also wanted far more involvement by broadcasters and producers from the region. 'Programme organizers' became heads of services and 'programme assistants' became producers, new titles chosen to suit the new duties. The responsibility was brought down to the level of production. Whereas programme organizers had always been English nationals, now they could be recruited from amongst the LOTE[23] language experts. John Tusa's era encouraged more professional journalism. Interviewing officials as well as opposition activists made for interesting radio debates in the early 1990s. New training methods encouraged the new style of journalism and taught producers how to make good use of all sources of information, and how to balance claims and counter-claims. Creating objective balanced programming became a technique that all producers had to master through learning the BBC's Producer Guidelines. These changes took place in the Persian and Pashto services.

Another important change was the technological advances in broadcasting. Digital recording meant much lighter equipment and much more mobility in the field for reporters. In 1983 there were no mobile phones in use. By 1992 almost all Mujahedin, even in the remotest mountains of Afghanistan, possessed either a satellite phone or a mobile. Producers could phone the warring sides in the middle of a battle and have them negotiate on air. In ten years much had changed in the style of journalism of the language services of the BBC and the Pashto Service was benefiting from these developments. The same editorial and production techniques were teaching producers how to make sensitive use of the LOTE languages of broadcasting.

During the 1990s the Persian Service also greatly increased its programmes about Afghanistan. Many of its producers, such as Baqer Moin, Behrouz Afagh and Massoumeh Torfeh, were amongst the first to travel to Afghanistan and to secure interviews with intellectuals, journalists and politicians. Dr Najibullah, the last of the pro-communist rulers of Afghanistan, gave one of his last interviews before his downfall to Massoumeh Torfeh in November 1991. While the Mujahedin ruled Afghanistan, the Persian Section became more prominent since most of the Mujahedin's top commanders would give interviews to the Persian rather than the Pashto Service. However, the most important single element that made BBC Persian and Pashto broadcasts indispensable for people inside Afghanistan was the fact that the international community had forgotten them during the years of civil war. With the departure of Soviet troops in 1989, and the collapse two years later of the Soviet Union, the US and much of the Western world lost interest in Afghanistan. President Najibullah, the last remaining communist leader, hung on to power for a further two years after the Soviet departure, but finally lost to the Mujahedin and was forced to step down in March 1992. The two years of Mujahedin government that followed meant war and bickering amongst the ethnic groups. The Pashtun forces of Gulbodin Hekmatyar (supported by Pakistan) fought fiercely to take power away from the Tajik forces of Burhanoddin Rabbani whose military commander was Ahmad Shah Massoud.

The combination of better journalism, more independence and improved technology meant that BBC Persian and Pashto broadcasts became the dominant sources of trusted information with regard to Afghanistan, and rivalries between the Pashto and Persian broadcasts began to surface.

It was during this period that the sensitivities about the use of Persian/Pashto increased. Listeners' letters often reflected a widespread perception that there was a difference between the reporting in the Persian and Pashto services and they accused the BBC of playing a double game. This could sometimes be explained through language accessibility of interviewees. For instance, during the war, the Pashto Section would tend to interview those who spoke Pashto while the Persian Section had access to both. Whereas most Afghan nationals speak Persian (Dari), many Dari speakers do not speak Pashto. It was not political choice or bias but journalistic practices and linguistic competencies that dictated such differences. Crawley, who was the Head of the Eastern Service for over ten years, recalls how sensitive the use of language was in the broadcasts, and how this 'affected attitudes' and 'caused tension' and criticism from both sides.[24]

The third stage: 1994–2001

Pakistan's ISI and the CIA had funded most Mujahedin groups during the years of anti-Soviet fighting. After the departure of the Soviet troops, Mujahedin governments, engaged in constant heavy in-fighting, soon proved ineffective and civil war continued. Pakistan became the main player and Pashtun-based groups that had been funded by the ISI tried to defeat the government, set up by the Tajik-dominated groups led by Rabbani and Ahmad Shah Massoud. According to Ahmad Rashid, it was at this stage that the 'CIA handed over its Afghan policy to its main allies in the region, Pakistan and Saudi Arabia'.[25] As such the Taliban were supported by the ISI to fill in the critical power vacuum that had been created by the in-fighting amongst the Mujahedin. The Taliban soon consolidated into a successful military force, seizing Khandhar as their capital and then making deals with Mujahedin leaders across the country. The only leader who would not make deals was Ahmad Shah Massoud, who continued to hang on to power in the north Badakhshan region. He set up home in Tajikistan and received support from those opposed to the Taliban such as Russia and Iran. The Taliban, which increasingly strengthened their ties with al-Qaeda, used Afghanistan as a training ground for making an army of terrorists.

Afghanistan again became a fighting ground between the Pashtun Taliban and the Tajik Ahmad Shah Massoud who, by this time, was the main leader of the Northern Alliance.

As such the BBC Persian and Pashto broadcasts continued to be indispensable. Details of Taliban advances and the fighting between Massoud and the Taliban were of vital importance to the people in the dominantly Pashtun provinces (south and east) or Tajik and Hazareh (north-east, north-west and central) in Afghanistan. They could best be heard in the Persian and Pashto broadcasts of the BBC. During the Taliban era the Pashto Section became far more important since it had access to all Pashto-speaking (and Urdu-speaking) Taliban. Few Taliban representatives would speak to the Persian Section, not because they did not want to but simply because they did not speak Dari. Thus the Persian broadcasts were mainly dominated by the voices of the Mujahedin who were mostly Tajik or Hazareh, both speaking Dari. Taliban statements would of course be written in but the voices that were heard were different in the two radios. Yet the Persian Section held its authority. So the BBC was often accused of towing two lines. With the Taliban there was also some gender discrimination since they refused to speak to female broadcasters. As Rashid has argued, the Taliban, drawn mainly from the southern Pashtun tribes of Afghanistan, 'galvanised Pashtun nationalism and revived hopes that once again the Pashtuns would dominate Afghanistan'.[26]

As such it was surprising that in late 1994 the BBC Head of the Eurasia Region, David Morton, decided to combine the two sections and create the BBC Persian & Pashto Service, headed by Baqer Moin, an Iranian. Could there have been a political reason for joining the two services, a preferred line coming from the FCO? Baqer Moin refutes such a suggestion, saying 'there was no political reason whatsoever'.[27] Moin's argument was that Persian-speaking people of Iran, Afghanistan and Tajikistan could benefit equally from the broadcasts. After all, during the early 1990s, following the break-up of the Soviet Union, Tajikistan had also joined the Persian-speaking world and the Persian Section was highly involved in reporting on crucial developments in this Central Asia country.[28] In 1990 the Communist-led government had been toppled in Tajikistan too and the opposition was keen to stress its historical ties with the Persian language and Persian culture. Thus it could be argued that the BBC Persian Service played a crucial role in bringing the Persian-speaking nations closer to each other. Later, Tajiks also began insisting on having their own 'unique Tajiki' accent distinguished from Persian. Experts, however, insisted that the Persian language was the same and that the BBC broadcasts were differentiated by language, not by country.

It could also be argued that the rivalry between Persian and Pashto broadcasters improved the content and that listeners were the real beneficiaries. This was a most exciting time for reporting events in Afghanistan. All political players approached the BBC. Everyone wanted to be heard on the BBC including the listeners whose voices were by this time a regular feature of all news and current affairs programmes. This all made for good radio.

Furthermore, the BBC's role was enhanced when the Taliban came to power since they began their own abuse of media freedom. During 1995–2001 the Taliban's unstructured, auto-cratic form of government reduced Afghanistan's media to four or five Taliban-run newspapers and a Taliban radio station called Voice of Sharia, with only a tiny television and radio station run by the opposition Northern Alliance remaining. In areas run by the Taliban – about 90 per cent of the country – television was banned entirely. The Taliban's Voice of Sharia station was the leading domestic station among Afghan heads of household

– according to Intermedia research for 1997–8 – attracting a 50 per cent regular audience in Dari and Pashto combined. Slightly more listened to Pashto (44 per cent) than to Dari (37 per cent).[29] It had become compulsory to listen to Taliban radio if only to be sure of having information about their numerous Islamic restrictions and edicts.

However, BBC Persian & Pashto Service remained the only trusted source of news, information, live discussion and entertainment, as well as vital messages on health and mine awareness. Afghans were very news-hungry and they trusted the BBC; as the social anthropologist Andrew Skuse observed: 'Even the Taliban loved it.'[30] That contention gains support from a British Parliament memorandum on the BBC World Service relationship with the Taliban:

> There is evidence that the Taliban, including their leaders, were very keen listeners to the BBC World Service [Pashto broadcasts] themselves, despite the fact that they disapproved of the Service. Mullah Omar, the leader of the Taliban, gave his only broadcast interview to the World Service after hearing the interview with Tony Blair during the height of the crisis, proving that he was a regular listener.[31]

However, despite their frequent interviews with the Pashto Section, the BBC at times angered the Taliban too. The reporting of the destruction of the Bamyan statues of Buddha was one such incident. The Pashto Section heard from the Taliban that they were going ahead with the plan since the statues were 'against Islamic belief'. The BBC Persian and Pashto Service was inundated with telephone calls from listeners wanting to condemn such an act. In order to balance the reporting the Persian broadcasters tried to contact the Taliban. Although they did not have many Persian speakers, finally the Taliban foreign minister, Vakil Ahmad Motevakil, agreed to speak in broken Dari and confirmed the statues would be destroyed the next day.

However, the BBC office in Kabul was closed down and Kate Clark who had worked through the Taliban era was expelled. The reason given by the Taliban information minister, Qudratuallah

Jamal, for the closure of the BBC office was that the Pashto Service had broadcast an interview with Ashraf Ghani Ahmadzai – later finance minister of Afghanistan – in which he called the Taliban '*jahel*' (ignorant) for destroying the Bamyan, saying it was 'un-Islamic'.[32] Nevertheless, the BBC was not banned, perhaps because all the 'soldiers were addicted to it'.[33]

Incidents such as this, or the news of the killing of the Mujahedin's iconic leader, Ahmad Shah Massoud, by terrorists posing as cameramen just two days before 9/11, made the BBC a unique household brand for the people of Afghanistan. The fact that the BBC Persian and Pashto Service could focus on both Tajiks and Pashtuns of Afghanistan meant that the coverage of news and events, as well as the depth and breadth of discussion and debates, was comprehensive. However, the report of the BBC Board of Governors Consultative Group found that:

> It is noted that the Persian service faces a structural problem in providing a common service in a single language to audiences in different countries (Iran, Afghanistan and Tajikistan) with very different outlooks. The Persian service has explained its approach and the constraints on financial resources and local reporting with which it has to contend.[34]

After 9/11

In 2000 the clear indications that the Taliban and al-Qaeda were partners in creating an international army for terrorism based in Afghanistan were still receiving little attention abroad. Ahmad Rashid says that he wrote about this alliance in *Foreign Affairs* magazine and spoke about it in forums in Washington, 'but there was no visible change in US policy'.[35] By this time Afghanistan was not just a security threat: it was the world's worst humanitarian disaster zone. It was only with the al-Qaeda attack, first on Ahmad Shah Massoud in Afghanistan on 9 September 2001, and then on the World Trade Center on 11 September, that international attention on Afghanistan was revived after a decade of neglect.

Due to the total ban of television under the Taliban, it was assumed that the majority of people living in Afghanistan had not seen pictures or video of the devastation visited on New York and Washington by the hijacked plane attacks of 11 September. 'How do you imagine a 110-storey building collapsing if you haven't seen it?' exclaimed Najiba Kasraee of the BBC Persian and Pashto Service. This is when radio came into its own. In the remote mountainous regions of Afghanistan where people have no access to TV and electricity, a small battery-powered radio can do a lot. 'What we did was interview Afghans living in New York,' Najiba explained. 'One taxi driver we interviewed was there when it happened. He told us what he saw and how he dragged the injured away and we also had him describe the scale of things and how big the buildings were.'[36]

Najiba Kasraee had another journalistic scoop when she interviewed the British prime minister, Tony Blair, after 9/11. This was a revelation to many BBC broadcasters since previously the Prime Minister was always described as busy, rather than 'available for interviewing'. The BBC Persian and Pashto Service suddenly became very popular not just with British officials, but also with the US Administration who contacted it for interviews. This use of the BBC language services for political communication became frequent in the years that followed 9/11. The BBC Persian and Pashto Service managers enjoyed having the 'scoop' and the exclusive interviews. Behrouz Afagh, who at the time was the editor of Eurasia region, says the British and US governments 'understood suddenly that the BBC had huge audiences and was a center for knowledge about Afghanistan.'[37] He believes that at the time the politicians' detailed knowledge of Afghanistan was limited and although government officials made themselves available for interview, 'we made the interview as tough as possible'. Afagh stresses, however, that 'no one ever put any pressure on the BBC to toe a particular line [...] my job was totally journalistic and I have never played the diplomatic role'. Obviously, says Afagh, the Service itself was 'interested in getting interviews from high ranking officials who were directly involved in the developments in Afghanistan'.[38]

Moin believes that the authority that the BBC Persian and Pashto Service had built in the 1990s 'became useful' after 11 September.[39] He managed to get funding from the FCO for a special three-hour daily live programme focused only on Afghanistan immediately after 9/11. 'The BBC Persian and Pashto Service was the most established way to deliver the communication from the international community to Afghanistan,' says Moin, while reiterating that there was 'no influence or directives from the Government'. Moin received the 2002 Elizabeth R award for 'exceptional contribution to public service broadcasting' from the Commonwealth Broadcasting Association (CBA).

During the three months that followed 9/11 the BBC Persian and Pashto Service broadcast daily longer-than-usual interviews with top US and British military and political officials. Whereas the usual BBC news interview duration is three to five minutes maximum, some of the BBC Persian and Pashto Service interviews with selected officials in the period September 2001–March 2002 were for nine to ten minutes on a daily basis.[40] At Prime Minister's Questions in the House of Commons on 1 May 2002, Tony Blair said: 'I would join the MP [Eric Illsley] in paying tribute to the World Service, which does a magnificent job. I saw for myself in the interviews I did with Pashto radio how hugely important they were in getting a message through to ordinary people in that country.'[41]

So with shifting international interest FCO was prepared to pour more funds into the Service. As well as three hours of additional programming, plans were made to bring in the BBC Trust for training journalists in Afghanistan. With so much interest, the FCO also agreed to provide funds for enhancing production for 24-hour FM broadcasts to Afghanistan. The BBC World Service Trust – which is a non-government organization established by the BBC World Service to promote development through innovative use of the media – set up shop in Afghanistan's state television and radio station. Further, a team made up of the Pashto and Persian services, the BBC World Service Trust and a wide range of experts from BBC Technology, BBC Public Policy and the Afghan Education Project provided Radio Afghanistan with two fully equipped, self-operating studios, digital-editing equipment, computers and mini discs, satellite phones and other essential production equipment. It also opened a Media Resource Centre in Kabul.

In November 2003, the BBC World Service launched a new, dedicated schedule of programming for Afghanistan. BBC for Afghanistan included three-hour blocks of new programming in the key languages (Persian and Pashto, plus some English and Uzbek) at breakfast, lunchtime and evening every day. During the programme cycle, the blocks were repeated and supplemented by local and international music programming. This coincided with the opening of three new FM relays in Konduz, Faizabad and Pol e Khomri, in addition to the established FM relays in Kabul, Mazar e Sharif, Bamyan and Jalalabad, which had opened in eastern Afghanistan over the previous 18 months. The transmitter in Bamyan was powered by solar power. The BBC later launched further FM stations including Herat, Khost, Maimana, and Kandahar, by 2003.

So it could be argued that a complete restructuring and reshaping of programmes took place after 9/11. The BBC Persian and Pashto Service reverted to being the Persian Service while BBC for Afghanistan replaced the Pashto Service.

A decade on, BBC for Afghanistan is facing serious challenges from local media outlets. There has been a rapid development of private television and FM stations in Kabul and new brands continue to enter the market. Radio Arman – with a weekly reach in Kabul of over 72 per cent – and Tolo TV – with weekly audiences in Kabul of over 80 per cent – are seriously challenging the BBC's ability to maintain a mass audience in the long term.[42] Their national reach is 25.9 per cent and 32.3 per cent respectively.[43] Television is now widespread in urban areas: 89 per cent watch weekly; 83 per cent own a television; and there are over 70 channels. In 2008, Afagh suggested that for the moment the

BBC's future strategy for Afghanistan was to stay with radio, and he believed that, despite their evident success, the local media do not have the freedom that the BBC enjoys and cannot report as objectively.[44] Our last chapter will describe how things changed again in 2009 with the development of BBC television for the broad Persian-speaking world.

The media scene in Afghanistan is now far more developed and the local media seem to understand the needs of their audiences or at least cater to their tastes. The BBC remains popular for morning news and for its web stories, but far less for analysis and debate. However, some recent attempts at joint programming with Afghan TV and radio stations are increasingly the order of the day. It is no longer the BBC that dominates the media scene in terms of creative analytical broadcasting, but rather the local media that encourage the BBC to keep up. The BBC Persian and Pashto Service, which once received almost 80 per cent weekly audiences, now reaches 59 per cent of adults in Afghanistan. Listener numbers are higher in rural areas and in Persian (42.5 per cent) than Pashto (28.9 per cent). Despite attempts to increase female listeners – such as special women's programmes funded by the BBC Trust – statistics provided by the BBC indicate that listening is still higher amongst men (54 per cent). The BBC's own research concludes that 'as new brands continue to enter the market, it will be a big challenge for the BBC to maintain such a mass audience in the long term'.[45] BBC for Afghanistan and BBC PTV have tried over the past two years to increase audiences by joint programmes with the local media. A new radio debate series in 2012, *Afghanistan Speaks*, was produced in conjunction with a group of local radio stations, and in 2013 a separate major TV debate series, *Open Jirga*, was produced by BBC Media Action in conjunction with Radio TV Afghanistan (RTA).[46] This was a very successful joint venture broadcast from RTA with ideas for continued cooperation. However, BBC PTV failed to convince RTA to re-broadcast some of its programmes, although another increasingly influential channel, Yak TV, is re-broadcasting a BBC PTV programme at 11 pm, with very few viewers.

6

Culture Wars as Foreign Policy: BBC Persian Television and the Islamic Republic of Iran

It is evident that international communication channels can play a significant role in foreign policy. Sometimes this is done by signalling impending events to the enemy, sometimes by direct promotion of a nation's position on a political topic, and sometimes by enticing a foreign audience with forbidden cultural fruit. And at times, a channel can get caught up in large political issues when it appears to be at the centre of the storm.

This chapter explores the establishment of BBC Persian Television (BBC PTV). It illustrates how the development of BBC PTV was one of the main foci in the most recent escalation of tensions between Iran and Britain, as high-ranking officials in Iran accused the British government of planning a 'soft war' on Iran and considered BBC PTV to be the key instrument of that war. It also shows how, at another critical juncture, namely the protests after the disputed presidential election of June 2009, BBC PTV played a pivotal role in communicating information to Iranian audiences, how it was jammed, and how, in what appears to be an escalation of this culture war, its Iranian staff and their relatives have been intimidated, harassed and imprisoned, leading to a real collapse of diplomatic relations between the UK and the Islamic Republic of Iran. We take the story up to the June 2013 elections, which produced a very different but no less fascinating process.

Also in this chapter, we explore the development of Iran's international broadcasting capacity and its emergence as a powerful player in international communications. Much of Western public diplomacy has been predicated on the idea of a unidirectional flow of persuasive strategies from the West to the Middle East. The massive expansion of Islamic Republic of Iran Broadcasting (IRIB), the Islamic Republic's state broadcaster, and its multilingual radio and television channels, has radically altered the balance of power in international communication and greatly reduces the efficacy of a simplistic public diplomacy strategy.

Relations between Iran and Britain have gone through several crises since the revolution of 1979. After Ayatollah Khomeini's fatwa in February 1989 against the British writer, Salman Rushdie, relations were severed. During the pre-reform period of the 1990s relations were raised back to the level of *chargé d'affaires* and, as a result of intense behind-the-scenes diplomacy during the reform era of President Mohammad Khatami, relations were normalized after 1998. In 2001 the then foreign secretary Jack Straw became the first high-ranking British official to visit the Islamic Republic.

But since President Mahmoud Ahmadinejad came to power in 2005 there has been a sharp downward spiral of relations, mostly relating to concerns about Iran's nuclear programme and the ensuing punitive sanctions imposed by the United States and Europe. Iran has continued to deny it has military designs for its nuclear programme and the West has continued to disbelieve the claim. In October 2011, Britain imposed further sanctions on Iran, directly targeting the banking sector, especially the Central Bank of Iran. This was an unprecedented move that caused fury inside Iran since it would create obstacles for Iran's international transactions. Sanctions also targeted the powerful Revolutionary Guards and banned travel for those involved with the nuclear industry. In retaliation the Iranian Parliament voted on 27 November 2011 to downgrade relations with Britain, with deputies shouting 'death to Britain' and calling for the expulsion of the British ambassador, Dominic Chilcott. The Islamic Republic's Guardian Council, which vets all decisions by the parliament, approved the move the following day. One article of the bill prohibits Iranians abroad and in Iran from cooperating in any way with the British media. Any cooperation, including giving interviews to BBC Persian Television, now carries a two- to three-year prison sentence. On 29 November 2011, Islamist militants stormed the British Embassy in Tehran and the British Ambassador's residence and gardens in Gholhak, northern Tehran. Britain retaliated with the expulsion from Britain of the entire staff of the Iranian Embassy in London. Thus, at the start of 2013 there were no formal diplomatic relations between the two countries and, with increasing EU pressure on Iran and the profound currency devaluation of the *toman*, the situation was extremely tense.

BBC World Service shifts to television

As we have argued, the BBC World Service was built originally on an inherent structural conflict: the need to take account of the strategic priorities of the FCO while remaining true to the core news values of impartiality and truthfulness of the BBC as a whole. That tension has required it to walk a tightrope of practices in regard to a very complex region of the world. Our reading of the historical evidence suggests a battle hard fought by the BBC World Service against various attempts by the FCO to determine and structure its content. Latterly, its guarantee of independence is enshrined in the Broadcasting Agreement signed by the FCO and the BBC Trust, and governments of the day have come to believe that its global provision of high-quality journalism make it a central actor in Britain's public diplomacy.

By 2000, the global media market was extremely crowded and competitive. The BBC World Service had to function along-side new and expanding international broadcasting channels that include Al Jazeera in both Arabic and English, China Central Television (CCTV), Russian, French and German broadcasters and foreign-language channels from Iran (which will be discussed below). BBC research indicated that the number of radio listeners was dropping and audiences were switching to television as their main medium of acquiring information, especially news. It was evident that the World Service needed to catch up. Perhaps in preparation, ten radio services – mainly eastern European but also including the Thai service – were deemed no longer neces-sary to the process of democratization in these countries and were cut, allowing the budget to be diverted to the development of television.

The Middle East was central to the development of foreign-language radio broadcasting in the 1940s and so it was also the first region in the roll-out of World Service television, first in Arabic which was launched in March 2008, then in Persian. The Arabic Service rapidly gathered audiences and has expanded from a news-only to a full-service channel. Anecdotal evidence suggests a tussle between Al Jazeera and BBC Arabic for audi-ences, and for dominance of the screens in Tahrir Square in Cairo and in Benghazi, Libya, during the 2011 political uprisings in those countries. But that is the stuff of further research that cannot be developed here.

With regard to Iran, it appeared that there was no prospect of the BBC being allowed to establish an FM presence there in order to improve the range and quality of radio reception. But further, the research evidence suggested that television was 'increasingly the dominant means by which millions of Iranians receive their news, particularly in the evening'.[1] This was especially the case for younger Iranians and, given that 70 per cent of the popu-lation was under 30, this was a large chunk of the audience.

In addition, ex-President Khatami's notion of the 'dialogue of civilizations', a creative appropriation of Huntington's 'clash of civilizations' that presaged a cautious overture to the West and triggered the UN's 2001 Year of Dialogue of Civilizations, had been superseded by a far more militant anti-Western posture. Mahmoud Ahmadinejad was elected President in Iran in 2005 and was proving far more defiant than previous Iranian presidents in dealing with the West. The British government was becoming increasingly impatient in its dealings with Iran and was keen to establish better communication with Iranians, attempting to speak directly to foreign audiences in line with the new paradigm of public diplomacy. So the BBC was moved once again to centre stage in the relations between the two countries.

Behrouz Afagh, the then head of the BBC World Service Asia and Pacific region, presented a proposal which received FCO approval, and so BBC PTV was born with an annual budget of £15 million and a staff of 150. The aim was to build up good audience levels in all Persian-speaking countries; the BBC claims that by early 2013 there were an approximate 12 million viewers in Iran[2] and some 2 million in Afghanistan. But the channel had another clear objective when it was launched, which Afagh describes as 'setting out to redefine the standards in Persian language television, to introduce Persian audiences to modern ideas of television news, and to bring about a qualitative change in the Iranian media landscape.'[3]

Initially, there was a daily eight-hour service that broadcast from 1700 to 0100 local time in Iran.[4] The idea was to create a service that addressed the broader Persian-speaking world and the content was intended for audiences not only in Iran, but also in Afghanistan and the wider region including Tajikistan, in total around 100 million Persian speakers. This was a clearly different approach than the one fought for Afghan radio, as described in Chapter 5. By this time Afghanistan was a very important element in Britain's regional policy and the British government, being one of the main stakeholders in the international efforts toward Afghan reconstruction, wanted to ensure it had a direct channel of communication to the people of Afghanistan; so presenters such as Jamaluddin Mosavi and Najieh Gholami were brought in to support the Afghan focus.

The core of the broadcast schedule would be news, complemented by a mix of current affairs, features and documentaries, culture, science, business and arts programmes. But it could be argued that the eight hours of television was meant to make a cultural impact, the programmes covering new technologies in Click, and including a dubbed version of the popular car programme Top Gear and plentiful coverage of life in Britain. Everything was broadcast in Persian from a new newsroom purpose-built in the new John Peel Wing behind New Broadcasting House, part of the slow removal of the entire World Service from its iconic home in Bush House.

As Nigel Chapman, then director-general, said on the evening of the launch of BBC PTV, the World Service

> strives to be accurate, impartial, editorially independent, and balanced with the widest possible range of views about an issue – [and] projects Britain's values of trustworthiness, openness, fair dealing, creativity, enterprise and community. It believes this promotes interest in Britain around the world. These goals are achievable because the BBC is independent from any form of editorial control from Government.[5]

In relation to Iran, the BBC World Service recognizes that:

> Iran is an important global and regional country. What Iran says and does matters in so many areas – in world politics and culture, global trade and energy issues, in the search for stability in the Middle East to name a few of these areas. In that context we argue that it is vital that Iranians have access to reliable and independent sources of news and information and this new channel will add significantly to their choices [...] This is a BBC channel. It has the same aims and values as all the other BBC news outlets. We aim to be authoritative and impartial in our journalism. In this respect we want to hear from Iran's leaders, opinion-formers and citizens

where their views are relevant. This is something we have made clear to the authorities in Iran and we will do our best to facilitate this within our limited capabilities. We aim to be trusted for the accuracy, editorial independence and expertise of our journalism. We want to use the technology to become a trusted forum for the exchange of ideas across cultural, linguistic and national boundaries.[6]

Richard Sambrook, in his Editor's column on the BBC website on 14 January 2009, acknowledged the challenge that lay ahead:

The BBC is well respected by opinion formers within Iran and brand awareness is high – despite government media restrictions. Media freedom is severely limited – so we hope BBC Persian TV will build a following by providing free and independent news and information – the traditional role of the BBC World Service over the last 75 years – and provide a window for Iranian viewers to the rest of the world in an open and unbiased way. The Iranian authorities have been a little apprehensive about the launch, describing it as 'an illegal channel', refusing us permission to work within Iran and suggesting anyone found working for it will be arrested as a spy. However, we hope once they have seen the service they may recognise the independence and quality of the channel – and hopefully take part in its programmes.[7]

BBC PTV was to complement the well-established Persian radio and its well-regarded Persian online presence and have no adverse effect on other services. But things didn't quite work out that way, as will become evident.

Various waves of tests and interviews produced a cadre of young Iranian employees, many with direct and immediate journalistic experience in Iranian newspapers and broadcasting; some also had intimate experience of Iranian jails, where they had been sent for blogging or journalistic activities. Others were brought in from across the Iranian diaspora.

BBC PTV went live on 14 January 2009, after some considerable delay. The launch party that night, attended by Annabelle

Sreberny, was an emotional affair. There were stories of elderly men calling from Tehran to congratulate the new service and explaining what a delight it was to finally see the faces behind this important service. The young team seemed suddenly to realize the full significance of the new service and were rather overwrought.

BBC PTV had tried to negotiate with the Islamic Republic to open an office in Iran but was refused, although the domestic BBC News has maintained an office and a correspondent in Tehran for many years. The television channel was seen as different by the Islamic Republic, aimed as it was at domestic Iranian audiences, and so from the beginning BBC PTV faced the huge challenge of trying to cover events inside Iran with no correspondent inside the country nor any professional source of broadcasting images from there.

But not only was BBC PTV denied a base inside Iran. It was to be prevented from having any open cooperation with Iranians inside the country. Already in 2007 the BBC team that had gone to Tehran to negotiate access and to set up an office had been labelled MI6 spies by Mehdi Kallur, then Ahmadinejad's head of communications and senior advisor.[8] Well before the service went live, the Islamic Republic had warned Iranians not to coop-erate with the new channel. On 21 October 2008, Iranian Culture Ministry's Press Deputy's Office expressed its concern over 'the interventionist, opportunist and nation-dividing' activities of BBC Persian.[9] In this public announcement the BBC was accused of communicating 'with some people with security-related records' to 'make programmes about suspicious subjects', which was a 'clear action against the national interests of a country and any continuation of this trend shows the poor intentions of BBC's founders'. The Minister for Culture and Islamic Orientation, Mohammad-Hossein Safar-Harandi, not only banned the channel from operating in Iran, but also forbade Iranian journalists to work for foreign news media.

As we have already discussed, the IRGC regarded the launch of BBC PTV as announcing a 'soft war' against Iran and stated that 'considering the objectives of soft war against the Iranian people, the lie-broadcasting BBC channel which is funded by English intelligence services […] is aiming to interfere in Iran's internal affairs and this necessitates the vigilance of revolutionary forces.[10] Ali Asghar Ramezanpoor, the former communications chief to President Mohammad Khatami, believes that the Supreme Leader, Ayatollah Ali Khamenei, 'saw the BBC PTV as articulating the British Government's plan for confronting Iran'. Ramezanpoor noted that Khamenei personally listens to all the news from BBC PTV and then gives the relevant orders for dealing with the West so 'the policy about dealing with Britain and the West is formulated on the basis of the news from BBC PTV'.[11]

'Soft war' and Iran's international broadcasting provision

As described in Chapter 2, the notion of 'soft war' (*jang-e narm*) has been articulated by Ayatollah Khamenei and adopted by the Islamic Republic, especially the IRGC. It has been used to support the development of the international activities of IRIB, making Iran a significant player in international communications.

The Iranian response to BBC PTV can be seen as hypocritical since the Islamic Republic itself also funds an extensive programme of international broadcasting. This builds on a system inherited from the previous broadcasting structure of the Pahlavi regime, which had already established some international broadcasting in the 1950s under its state broadcaster NIRT. Indeed, radio broadcasting hours for a number of big international broadcasters in 1996 already counted IRIB as the seventh largest.

The Islamic Republic had slowly developed the infrastructure of IRIB to include extensive foreign-language broadcasting across a range of platforms, making it a significant regional player and a new voice in the raucous world of public diplomacy. Internally, it includes several publishing, film, electronic and research ventures, making it the key ideological vehicle of the Islamic Republic and the major actor within the Iranian cultural industries.

Interestingly, IRIB also calls its foreign-language broadcasts a 'world service', a direct crib of the BBC's name. Its website suggests that as of spring 2013 it currently broadcasts in 27 languages, including Hebrew. It has several Arabic language television channels including Al Alam, which is IRIB's 24-hour Arabic news channel, targeting a pan-Arab audience. It transmits on a number of satellites and can be received in Europe, the Middle East, Asia-Pacific and North America. IRIB's understanding of the world and its propaganda role are clearly articulated, if in rather awkward English:

> In the present age, employment of Radio and TV as two fast and at the same time accessible media serves as a social necessity. It is also considered as an inseparable part of the modern life. In fact, if any one is left behind, he/she would be totally omitted from the social life.[12]

The global expansion of international broadcasting channels is mainly driven by private interest and profit. But IRIB tends to see in them only statist projects intent on change in the region in military-style campaigns:

> The political and social changes of the recent years in the different parts of the world signify the outbreak of intensifying media war, focusing on winning the public opinion. It also concentrates on intended drastic changes in culture and life styles of the listeners and viewers, specifically in the Middle East. Hence, the active and effective presence of the Islamic Republic of Iran Broadcasting (IRIB) in this battle field requires the planning and intelligent management so that it would pave the ground for surmounting the obstacles as well as taking full advantage of opportunities to achieve its own goals.[13]

The media are seen as powerful and their messages impossible to resist. But despite the huge range of media channels in multiple languages broadcasting into the international ether, only some are deemed dangerous:

> Apparently at the status quo when the supranational waves and messages have trespassed the geographical and cultural borders, with domineering empire of Western Media aiming for the cultural conversion of the Independent nations specifically focusing on the Islamic Republic of Iran, IRIB should play its key role in strengthening the country's cultural solidarity as well as stressing national identity together with fighting against the destructive waves more than before, through complete preparation. The importance of the issue can be found in the Late Imam Khomeini (Rh)'s words: 'IRIB serves to be the country's public university.'[14]

Text on the website sets out 15 principles that govern IRIB content, including such lofty goals as indeed serving 'as a public university', 'saying welcome to criticism' and letting 'humanitarian talents flourish so that it would result in fertile imaginations and minds'. Given the pressures since 2009 on the university teaching of the social sciences, the limitations imposed in 2012 on women's access to various university subjects, the arrest and imprisonment of people expressing almost any kind of critical opposition and the arcane and convoluted processes to get permission to make films, record music or publish a book, such IRIB claims have a hollow ring. But they clearly echo the widespread position of the Islamic Republic of being involved in a fierce propaganda war with the West.

In 1997 the Sahar Universal Network (SUN) was set up as the international television network in Iran as part of the foreign broadcasting branch of IRIB. It broadcasts in English, French, Arabic, Bosnian, Urdu and other languages. The English department is responsible for providing the world with the latest news and programmes all in English. The Sahar website describes its purpose in hyperbolic and aggressive language:

> In the first decade of the twenty-first century, blatant hegemonic methods, such as the use of force and territorial expansion

no longer apply. The increase of various mass media has made psychological warfare, via propaganda and persuasion the best method of aggression from without and the new 'fifth column' from within, brainwashing citizens. Such media are able to penetrate anywhere and everywhere, irrespective of national borders. Thus, the mass media has metamorphosed into the most effective weapon ever devised in both the political and economic arenas.[15]

Sahar's mission, on the other hand, is:

- To introduce the Islamic Revolution of Iran to foreign viewers as the most significant, influential uprising of the past century by explaining Islam's views on politics and independence as well as its rejection of oppression as opposed to the nations' acceptance of oppression. The introduction includes the historical, social and political background [...] the reasons why the revolution occurred and the means used to gain victory, as well as the personality and views of Imam Khomeini.
- To strengthen solidarity and create an atmosphere of trust and understanding between Iranian Muslims and other nations by showing Iranian society as it really is, thus negating unfavourable propaganda generated by the Western media. To introduce the rich Iranian–Islamic culture, as well as the improvements and political, cultural, social and economic advances made by the Islamic Republic of Iran.
- To confront the influence of the non-Islamic culture in the world of Islam and reveal the hegemonic policies of the great powers, which wish to dominate the people and nations of the world.
- To inform and update world viewers on the news in Iran and the world at large, paying special attention to the Islamic world and liberal movements. The aim is to counter the misleading news dominated by the West and Zionism.[16]

Also under the aegis of the international broadcasting wing of IRIB, Al-Alam news network, set up in 2003, broadcasts television programmes to the Arabic-speaking world, while Al-Kawthar TV produces Arabic cultural and religious programmes, mainly designed to promote Shi'ism.

Since 2005 the Islamic Republic has been funding Press TV to 'take revolutionary steps as the first Iranian international news network, broadcasting in English on a round-the-clock basis'. Its self-description also makes large claims. The vision of Press TV is:

- heeding the often neglected voices and perspectives of a great portion of the world
- embracing and building bridges of cultural understanding
- encouraging human beings of different nationalities, races and creeds to identify with one another
- bringing to light untold and overlooked stories of individuals who have experienced the vitality and versatility of political and cultural divides firsthand.[17]

Press TV's London operation has delighted in employing British journalists and figures out of favour with mainstream British opinion, including Andrew Gilligan, George Galloway (elected MP for Bradford West in March 2012) and Yvonne Ridley (who converted to Islam after being held hostage in Afghanistan), to mock the British government and feast on British social issues. Press TV presents its coverage as novel, although such topics are present within British media itself. More insidious is its advertising slogan of 'presenting the other opinions' (itself an echo of Al Jazeera's most famous programme) which has been rendered ludicrous by the even tighter ideological controls imposed on all forms of expression inside Iran, but especially print media, after the June 2009 presidential campaign and the 'stolen election'. Clearly, there is one rule about free speech for Iranians but another for the rest of the world.

In November 2011, Press TV was threatened with a revocation of its licence in the UK. The channel had aired an interview with Maziar Bahari, a previously imprisoned *Newsweek* journalist, that had been conducted under duress while he was imprisoned in Iran.[18] This had been deemed a serious breach of the Broadcasting Code and resulted in Ofcom imposing a £100,000 fine on Press TV Limited. In this process, the Ofcom licensee (Press TV Limited, based in London) made representations that suggested that editorial control of the channel rested with Press TV International (based in Tehran), while UK broadcasting rules require that a licence is held by the person who is in general control of the TV service: that is, the person that chooses the programmes to be shown in the service and organizes the programme schedule. Ofcom gave Press TV Limited the opportunity to apply to have its operations in Tehran correctly licensed by Ofcom and offered to assist it in doing so. Press TV Limited was also given the opportunity to make representations on Ofcom's 'minded to revoke' letter. Press TV Limited failed to make the necessary application and so, in January 2012, Ofcom revoked Press TV's licence to broadcast in the UK.

Press TV's response was somewhat bizarrely to blame 'members of the royal family and government' and Ofcom officials who were 'influenced by powerful pro-Israeli politicians and US sympathisers'. Press TV has been under further investigation for publishing a number of unsubstantiated reports about the shooting down of US drone planes in Somalia for which no clear evidence has been provided. In October 2012, the European satellite provider Eutelsat SA stopped carrying a number of Iranian satellite channels, including Press TV and some other IRIB channels, following an order from the European Commission, following months of jamming of television channels by the Islamic Republic.

In short, the Islamic Republic supports a large infrastructure of international broadcasting that is directly state-funded and state-supervised to broadcast abroad its vision of the world. IRIB is not only a domestic but also an international broadcaster and the pre-eminent definer and disseminator of the ideology of the Islamic Republic. This might make it harder for Iranian officials to understand the unique, nuanced and contested relationship between the FCO and the BBC World Service. It is ironic that the Islamic Republic lambasts external voices as waging 'soft war' when its own rhetoric stokes the fires of this process and when the disjunction between its internal and external approaches is so transparent.

But it is evident that BBC PTV was in the regime's political sights from the start. In January 2009, a few hours before the commencement of BBC PTV programmes, Gholam Hossein Mohseni Ejei, who was at the time the intelligence minister, expressed concern over the channel's activities and claimed that 'BBC Persian TV is not appropriate for the country's security'.[19] The head of IRIB, Ezzatollah Zarghami, also reacted to the new television channel. Both denied that BBC PTV 'could have any effect on Iranian people's view about their own society and their worldview', but also accused the channel of 'making divisions between people and ruining their trust'.[20]

Over the next few months, this rhetoric would escalate until, once again, the BBC was embroiled in a major political incident in Iran: the coverage of the run-up to the June 2009 presidential election and its aftermath. Thus while other British organizations have been the target of the wrath of the Islamic Republic, including the British Council,[21] none has endured more angry rhetoric and attempts to limit their operations than BBC PTV. It could also be said that all news broadcasters, including CNN, Al Jazeera and others, thrive on the coverage of war and conflict, so that the contested election and its powerful and latterly violent aftermath was a kind of gift to the fledgling channel that enabled it to show its real ability and worth.

The 2009 presidential election and the international media

The Islamic Republic's legitimacy is based on two pillars: the rule of the Supreme Jurist (*Velayat-e Faghih*) and the popular mandate of the 1979 revolution, so there has always been a strong attempt to maintain mass participation in elections. The build-up to the June 2009 presidential elections was no different.[22]

Over 450 candidates, including women who are technically disallowed from being elected President, put their names forward. The Guardian Council selected four: Mahmoud Ahmadinejad, the incumbent; Mohsen Rezaee, a former Commander of the IRGC and then secretary of the Expediency Council; Mehdi Karroubi, a former Speaker of the Majlis; and Mir-Hossein Mousavi, the last prime minister of Iran. Social media that had previously been banned were suddenly available and every candidate, including Ahmadinejad, put up a Facebook page. Football stadia, previously out of bounds to women, became the location for huge rallies and, for the first time under the Islamic Republic, a woman – Zahra Rahnavard, Mir-Hossein Mousavi's wife – addressed the mixed crowds. Candidates also produced posters, flags, bandanas and other accoutrements of what looked more and more like an American presidential process. Cleverly but somewhat serendipitously, the Mousavi camp selected green – the colour of Islam, of the environment, of peace – so that Ahmadinejad's followers wrapped themselves in the nationalist symbolism of the flag.

The international media were welcomed and not only BBC PTV but also domestic BBC ran stories, John Simpson milling in the political crowds to report from the streets of Tehran while Channel 4's Lindsey Hilsum showed how lively the political mood was even outside Tehran. On the day of the election, huge queues formed at polling stations, people wrote of the difficulties in being able to place their votes and hours were extended in some places. But within a couple of hours of the polls closing, despite ballot boxes having to be collected and votes having to be counted by hand and despite large numbers of diasporic Iranians voting from abroad, Ahmadinejad was declared the winner with 65 per cent of the vote.

The period after 9 June was the most politically volatile since the revolution. By the end of that evening, Iranians in many cities were gathered in the streets talking about a 'stolen election'. Just days after the vote, demonstrations of millions of people took place in Tehran, Isfahan, Shiraz and elsewhere, rivalling those of 1979. Facebook rapidly went 'green', with people altering their images to include a bright green 'Where is my Vote?'. The international media, there to cover the election, discovered a powerful new story. John Simpson's reports for domestic BBC channels were used by BBC PTV so Iranians at home could see the kind of coverage their public outcry was receiving. International media, including BBC PTV, also broadcast significant amounts of user-generated content sent from the streets of Tehran and elsewhere. This was vetted by BBC PTV's social media experts for veracity, as far as that was possible in a fast-moving situation. Given the lack of coverage of the demonstrations by IRIB, it was little surprise that viewers welcomed the ongoing serious coverage by BBC PTV.

The regime responded. Ahmadinejad likened the popular response to fans seeing their team lose a football match and that it was meaningless, all *'khas o khashak'*, dust and motes. Within hours, video responses and songs declaring that he was himself *khas o khashak* flooded the net. The regime reacted in many ways, clamping down with violence on the internal dissent, trying to control internet use, but also suddenly terminating the visas of international media and disallowing them access. Slowly the media bubble burst and reporters left the country. But mobile phone images, blogged stories, Twitter messages and videos with musical scores on YouTube all leaked out of the country to eager members of the Iranian diaspora, who circulated them widely or directly to the international media channels. The diaspora also staged demonstrations and teach-ins in numerous locations around the world. And the international response was enormous: Joan Baez recorded 'We shall overcome' in Persian, U2 turned their concert green and there were many other kinds of solidarity. The speed of the populace's responses, their creativity and digital skills were unprecedented for any political movement.

But regime discourse rapidly connected these events to its perceived struggle against 'soft war', despising the internal political dynamic of the response to blame external manipulation. Soon after the elections, on 9 July 2009, Esmaeel Ahmadi Moghaddam, the Chief of Police, described what happened after the presidential election as the enemy's effort to attack the Islamic Republic in a soft war: 'to portray the regime as inefficient, to disappoint people, to attract people inside Iran and finally to demolish the regime and put in place the western liberal democratic values'.[23] A number of British Embassy staff were arrested after the demonstrations and accused of spying and working against national security; many spent time in prison.

On 31 August 2009, in a meeting with some university professors, Ayatollah Khamenei called the crisis after the elections a 'determining political examination' and said that the crisis was a 'war' with university professors who are 'officers in the soft war battle field'.[24] About a month later (5 October 2009) the Armed Forces' General Headquarters announced that a special taskforce had been set up to study different aspects of the 'soft war'.[25] In a speech to the Basij militia on 25 November 2009, Khamenei stressed that 'confronting the enemy's soft war is the main priority of the Islamic Republic'.[26] He called on the Basij militia and all the state media to be vigilant, saying that 'the enemy aims to create divisions and distrust in society through sophisticated cultural and communications tools'. Soon afterwards, the Head of Intelligence and Operations of the Armed Forces reiterated that the priority in the fourth decade of the Islamic Revolution was confronting the 'soft threat' which he described as 'influencing a nation's beliefs through provocation of public thoughts, smear campaigns, exaggeration, dissemination of wrong information, strike and sanction, civil disobedience and boycotting the elections'.[27]

While from the start there had been almost constant low-level antagonism between the Islamic Republic and the new television channel, after the 2009 election various moments triggered more extreme responses from the regime, all framed in its 'soft war' rhetoric.

The death of Neda Agha Sultan

The huge demonstrations in Tehran and elsewhere after the election amassed the largest crowds seen on Iranian streets since the revolution of 1979. While they started peacefully, different kinds of violence started to occur, including sniper fire on demonstrators from upper storeys of buildings. A mobile-phone-captured video of Neda Agha Sultan, a 27-year-old student who was shot dead during a rally on 20 June 2011, was disseminated worldwide, broadcast on many television channels and uploaded on to YouTube where, in a number of differently sound-tracked versions, it has been viewed by literally millions.

One response by Islamic Republic officials was to claim that the BBC had killed Neda. A couple of weeks after her death, Zarghami, the head of IRIB, called the video 'phony' and said that 'Venezuela's ambassador was also saying that in the second round of elections in their country, a scenario like this lady [Neda] was carried out to pretend that Chavez's votes were falsified but they did not succeed'. He added that 'BBC and CNN aired this phony picture and then a man called Arash Hejazi made a big fuss over it and there is no trace of him now'.[28] Bijan Nobaveh, a former IRIB reporter at UN headquarters in New York and now an elected Majlis MP, called the video an 'artistic masterpiece' of cultural activity in the 'soft war'.[29] Several scenarios were suggested by Islamic Republic officials to justify Neda's murder and some directly implicated BBC PTV. *Javan* newspaper, an affiliate of the IRGC, claimed that a BBC correspondent in Iran had employed some thugs to kill Neda to make the video.[30] Later on, in an interview with *Newsweek*, President Ahmadinejad claimed that Neda was killed after the filming and the BBC had directed the video.[31] A documentary on Neda made by BBC PTV later showed how the young doctor who had tried to save Neda had himself gone into exile to escape the regime. In fact, he came to London and was interviewed in detail by BBC PTV, giving the Islamic Republic another excuse to blame this entire episode on the BBC.

The broadcasting of the story of Neda did re-establish the power and immediacy of big media over Facebook, Twitter and other forms of communication. Mehdi Khalaji, once a religious trainee in Qom but now based at the Washington Institute for Near East Policy, has described the broadcast power of the images of Neda:

> After Neda there was a flood of impact-making pictures and reports. The mentality changed; that is, the level of trust in the government by the governed – and the growth of trust in Western media to tell it as it is. Even many of the clergy in Qom and Najaf went out and bought satellite dishes after Neda. They no longer trusted the Iranian government or state TV.[32]

Jamming

One of the first regime responses to the new television channel had been jamming. Jamming or blocking signals and access was itself nothing new for the Islamic Republic. The BBC Persian website has been blocked from January 2006 and only been inter-mittently available since then, although inside Iran there is no shortage of adept filter-breakers and hackers who share how to gain access. Similarly, one of the first responses to BBC PTV was to try to prevent the signal from finding its audience.

The BBC's first official reaction to jamming its Persian pro-grammes was a day after the controversial presidential elections, 12 June 2009. The BBC said that 'the satellites it uses to broad-cast in Persian were being jammed from Iran [...] which had become "progressively worse".[33] The jamming affected other channels such as BBC Arabic Television as well. BBC World Service director Peter Horrocks said that 'any attempt to block BBC Persian television is wrong and against international treaties on satellite communication. Whoever is attempting the blocking should stop it now.' He added that 'it seems to be part of a pattern of behaviour by the Iranian authorities to limit the reporting of the aftermath of the disputed election.[34]

Soon afterwards, the BBC increased the number of satellites that carry its BBC Persian programmes, but it was difficult for
audiences to easily access the broadcasts.[35] In August 2010, French
regulators asked the International Telecommunication Union
(ITU) to intervene after numerous unsuccessful communications over the issue with Iran. The jamming heightened during the
coverage of the death of leading reformist cleric Grand Ayatollah
Hossein Ali Montazeri in December 2009.[36] Again during BBC
PTV's exclusive interview with Hillary Clinton on 26 October 2011
and at other moments, Iranian locals reported severe jamming.
Of course, access to email and the internet is similarly blocked
at times. Sadegh Saba of BBC PTV has appeared at hearings in
the EU, demanding that the international community react more
seriously at these attempts to limit and censor international broadcasters, but as yet there has been no coordinated response. As a
result of jamming, BBC PTV has continuously moved between
different satellite platforms, which has made it hard for Iranians
to find its signal and has seriously reduced its audience. In 2012,
the BBC hosted a seminar on international broadcasting without
barriers at which Eutelsat and Arabsat representatives described
the increase in jamming that stemmed mainly from China and
Iran,[37] while a report on the topic has set out the possible medical
consequences of jamming on the host population.[38]

Earlier, in January 2010, the Iranian Intelligence Ministry
had published a list of 60 organizations that it accused of inciting
the post-election unrest and of being involved in the 'soft war'
being waged against Iran.[39] The list included the Open Society
Institute established by George Soros, Human Rights Watch,
Freedom House and Yale University. Persian-language media,
including RFE/RL's Radio Farda, VOA and Radio Zamaneh,
based in the Netherlands, were also singled out. BBC PTV was
among them. The Foreign Affairs deputy of the Intelligence
Ministry announced that any collaboration with these organizations was illegal and would be considered a crime.

The coverage of a number of incidents in Iran, including the
invasion of student dormitories in Tehran and an interview with an

economist critical of Ahmadinejad's policies, all triggered further commentary about the supposedly nefarious role of BBC PTV.

Khamenei documentary

On 17 September 2011, BBC PTV aired a documentary about Iran's Supreme Leader, Ayatollah Khamenei,[40] that triggered a great deal of response. Strong satellite jamming started as soon as the programme began, so that during the airing, Iranian audiences could hardly watch the programme.[41] On 19 September it was reported that six documentary film-makers (Mojtaba Mirtahmasb, Hadi Afarideh, Katayoon Shahabi, Shahnam Bazdar, Nasser Saffarian and Mohsen Shahnazdar) had been arrested in Tehran, allegedly for cooperating with BBC PTV.[42] These only added to the list of already jailed film-makers including Mohammad Rasoulof and Jafar Panahi, who is kept under house arrest. All the film-makers protested that they had had nothing to do with the making of the documentary and Sadegh Saba, the head of BBC PTV, vehemently denied any connection between these film-makers and BBC PTV. He added that the BBC had sought no help from inside Iran for making the Khamenei documentary.[43] Two of the film-makers (Nasser Saffarian and Mohsen Shahnazdar) were released on 9 October 2011 and Mirtahmasb was released in November, but the rest are still under arrest.[44] As a direct consequence of these arrests, many international film directors withdrew their films from the Cinema Verite film festival that was scheduled in Tehran for early November 2011.[45]

The director Samuel Sebastian wrote:

> I find it particularly outrageous that Iran's regime tortures and prevents the work of my fellow filmmakers and, at the same time, organizes a film festival, ironically called 'Cinema Verite' and in which Iranian filmmakers have no right to participate, even they don't have the right to make movies, which I know is as if I'd lost the right to see, to feel, to talk and, of course, the right to express freely.[46]

The regime's direct response claimed that:

> we are well aware that such decisions have been made under pressure from the Zionist Lobby dominating most of Europe and America; because they are desperately seeking to divert public attention away from the economic crisis in Europe and the Wall Street Occupy movement in American [*sic*].[47]

Jafar Panahi, along with Nasrin Sotoudeh, the lawyer, was awarded the Sakharov Prize in November 2012, while the 2011 film *This is not a Film*, made by Panahi and Mojtaba Mirtahmasb, was nominated for the 2013 Oscars. Panahi's later 2013 film, *Closed Curtain*, about two people trying to evade state security and taken as an allegory of his own condition, won a prize at the Berlin Film Festival; in July 2013, Panahi was invited to become a member of the Academy of Motion Picture Arts and Sciences.

The Intelligence Ministry followed up the arrests of the filmmakers by declaring in a public announcement that affiliates of an illegal network that were providing information to the intelligence services of the 'old colonialist', under the cover of working with the BBC, had been arrested. The announcement said that 'the secret network were receiving significant amounts of money through secret channels and complicated money laundering systems, normally used by espionage services. This was to deliver operations that were commanded by the psychological operations centre of England's intelligence services which is called the BBC'.[48] Ramezanpoor has argued that one of the aspects that most annoyed the Iranian state authorities about BBC PTV was that it recruited more staff from the wave of Iranian journalists who left Iran because of the brutal crackdown after the 2009 contested presidential election.[49]

The internal tension over BBC PTV became public when the ruling conservatives accused the opposition reformists of sending their operatives to BBC PTV and VOA to encourage dissent.[50] The editor of the conservative *Resalat* newspaper claimed that 'now the main producers of the enemy's voice [BBC PTV and VOA TV] are the reformists of *dovom khordad*' ['Second of

Khardad', a reference to Khatami supporters]. Hojat ul-Islam Heidar Moslehi, the Iranian Intelligence Minister, repeatedly warned people against cooperating with the BBC and called BBC operations a cover for the British intelligence services. He called the BBC's request for the involvement of British and even American governmental organizations a clear violation of BBC claims of neutrality and independence and suggested that: 'BBC is not a media. It is just an organisation that uses media-work as a cover but its identity is Zionist-Baha'i and its mission is political intelligence.'[51]

Seyyed Mohammad Hosseini, the Minister of Culture and Islamic Guidance, responded to a question about the arrest of the documentary makers by saying that 'any cooperation with channels like BBC Persian was seen as an intention to topple the regime and the person was to be considered a dissident'. Ahmadi Moghaddam, the Chief Commander of Police Forces (*Nirooy-e-Entezami*), said that the VOA and the BBC were extensions of American intelligence services such as the CIA and cooperation with these channels would be treated as cooperation with foreign intelligence services: 'Cooperation with these channels is not a media activity but is cooperating with the enemies' intelligence services and therefore the Iranian Intelligence Ministry is monitoring and taking necessary actions.'[52]

The Voice of America, organized by the US Broadcasting Board of Governors, is a competitor to BBC PTV for Iranian audiences, but it adopts a clearly 'oppositional' position to the Islamic Republic. BBC PTV aims to provide fair and balanced coverage but has found it very hard to access regime spokesmen to provide their opinions. In regime eyes, there is no evident distinction between the two. Nor, in regime eyes, can the BBC World Service be separated from British intelligence and British foreign policy. Even if all our research suggests the BBC's ongoing desire to maintain editorial independence, this is unlikely to change such entrenched opinion in Tehran.

Colonel Ramezan Sharif, the head of the Islamic Republic Guard Corps (*Sepah*), argued that in their comments about the arrests of the six film-makers, the 'enemy' was trying to divert other nations' attention from the Islamic Revolution and the Islamic Republic model by propagating their message through channels such as the BBC.[53] He added that the BBC uses different experts and an extensive archive to portray the Islamic Republic as unsuccessful.

Following the official reactions about the connection between Iranian documentary makers and BBC PTV, the Head of House of Cinema (an institute based in Tehran which promoted Iranian-made films) wrote a letter to the Documentary Film Association warning them that cooperation with Persian-speaking channels outside Iran is illegal. He wrote: 'the enemy's media empire, in their soft war with the Islamic Republic of Iran, is trying to damage our country's national, cultural and religious values through Farsi-speaking channels outside Iran.'[54] In his letter he mentions legal articles that are related to crimes against national and international security of the country, and also gathering and plotting these crimes. The letter clearly says that these laws will be violated in a case of working with aforementioned channels. This reaction happened after two announcements by the House of Cinema had condemned the arrests. After their publications, the pressure on House of Cinema increased and Mohammad Mehdi Asgarpour, the head of House of Cinema, later said in a press conference that his organization would support the film-makers until their court proceedings. While accusing the BBC and the VOA of being led by Baha'is, he also criticized the lack of sufficient legislation against working with foreign media and called the current situation 'unclear' about the legal status of such cooperation.[55] The House of Cinema had been established as a civil society organization in 1989 to promote the Iranian film industry and had more than 20 affiliated organizations; it was ordered to be closed in January 2012 by Mohammed Hosseini, the Minister of Culture.

At around the same time, the US Broadcasting Board of Governors (BBG), which oversees the broadcasts of Radio Farda and VOA radio and television, together with the BBC, protested against 'an escalating campaign by the Iranian government to silence independent media in Iran', referring to the arrests, satellite jamming and internet disruptions on their web pages.[56] In addition to these issues, Peter Horrocks, the director of BBC Global News, noted that:

> Iranian police and officials have been arresting, questioning and intimidating the relatives of BBC staff. We believe that the relatives and friends of around 10 BBC staff have been treated this way. Passports have been confiscated, homes searched and threats made. The relatives have been told to tell the BBC staff to stop appearing on air, to return to Iran, or to secretly provide information on the BBC to the Iranian authorities.[57]

He connected this harassment with BBC PTV's documentary about Khamenei.

Ramezanpoor, who used to be Khatami's chief of communications and is now a regular commentator on BBC PTV, has suggested that the BBC's contact with Iran has diminished drastically due to the general fear of speaking with the BBC. He said that the Iranian authorities have refused to be interviewed by the channel and have intentionally reduced the information they provide so that the BBC and other international sources cannot gather detailed information:

> The policy has been to weaken all international media and this has succeeded. Now BBC PTV's only sources are opposition living abroad. The only Iranian sources remaining are the websites close to ayatollah Khamenei, IRGC and Ahmadinejad. Everything else is closed down and blocked. As a result, without a reporter inside Iran and without access to accurate internal information BBC PTV has become much weaker in reporting the news.[58]

The problem of lack of access makes the work of BBC PTV difficult, but creativity and zeal compensate, evident in their coverage of the 2013 election, which we describe shortly.

A changing media ecology in Iran

BBC PTV was the first major external television broadcaster into Iran. But much has changed since 2009, in a quite radical transformation of the Iranian mediascape.

The television channel Farsi 1 which operates out of the Hong Kong-based headquarters of Star TV, a subsidiary of Murdoch's News Corp, launched in August 2009. News Corp owns half the channel, the other half being owned by Saad Mohseni, the chairman of the Moby Group based in Kabul. It broadcasts popular Korean, Colombian and US shows and also dubs them into Persian rather than using subtitles, making them more broadly accessible. Farsi 1's more daring fare includes the US series *Prison Break*, *24* and *Dharma and Greg*, and it has also shown *Body of Desire*, a steamy Spanish-language telenovela.

It has also has been targeted, not as an actor in a 'soft war' but as a Zionist carrier of corrupt Western culture. The prominent hard-line magazine *Panjereh* (Window) devoted an issue to Farsi 1, featuring on the cover a digitally altered version of an evil-looking Murdoch sporting a button in the channel's signature pink and white colours. 'Murdoch is a secret Jew trying to control the world's media, and [he] promotes Farsi 1,' the magazine declared. 'Farsi 1's shows might be accepted in Western culture [...] but this is the first time that such things are being shown and offered so directly, completely and with ulterior motives to Iranian society. Does anybody hear alarm bells?' wrote Morteza Najafi, a regular *Panjereh* contributor.[59] Satellite dishes are not strictly legal, although their possession and use is widespread and sporadic action is sometimes taken with police confiscating dozens of dishes. Some Iranians blame the state channels for the exodus of viewers, saying they should make more appealing shows. Mohammad-Taghi Rahbar, a Member of Parliament, in an interview with the Iranian news agency IWNA, said: 'Satellite TV programs such as those broadcast on Farsi 1 destroy the chastity and honor of our families and encourage the young to take up lovemaking, wine drinking and Satan worship [...] The channel is funded by "Zionist money" and planned and managed by Iran's enemies [...] What family that has any dignity would let its members watch Farsi 1?'[60]

MTN was established in 2009 as a platform from 'which to develop and launch a series of new television channels that would aim to set the highest benchmark for quality, innovation and entertainment for a Persian speaking audience.'[61] Its first television channel, Manoto TV, launched in 2010 and its main contribution to altering the Iranian television environment was to stage a live singing contest recorded in London called Googoosh's Music Academy, building on the huge reputation of the Iranian diva. The programme was extremely popular and this has been followed up by an Iranian version of the ITV format *Come Dine with Me*. GEM is another Iranian television newcomer, offering mainly dubbed versions of high-end Turkish soap operas, a format that has proved surprisingly popular. And beyond the new commercial players offering a wide variety of entertainment programming, the state-supported stations of the Russians, the Chinese, the French and the Germans now also offer international broadcasts in Persian. So the entire media ecology of Iran has changed considerably, and there are many competitors for audiences with BBC PTV.[62]

Indeed, Iranian state television itself has diversified in a general attempt to attract youth and other audiences with a range of channels that focus on football, sports, fashion, gossip, music and entertainment, content that is broadly non-political – although each of these areas has in its own way become politicized at some point under the Islamic Republic.[63]

So various political and cultural struggles are being played out across Iranian television channels. The young Iranians who competed so valiantly to be employed by BBC PTV might not have fully understood – or been able to anticipate – the consequences for their own well-being and safety of joining the organization. As a consequence, most are unable and unwilling to travel to Iran and have become *persona non grata* in their own country. While BBC PTV is not the only British – or only media – institution to be accused of espionage and cultural warfare, it has been at the centre of the storm which does not look as though it will abate any time soon.

Indeed, late 2011–12 saw worsening relations between Britain and Iran. In November 2011, 'students', widely thought to be IRGC and Basij, suddenly attacked the British Embassy compound in Tehran, causing considerable damage and injuring some staff. The Embassy was closed, the Ambassador returned to Britain and formal diplomatic relations with Iran were severed, making travel in and out very difficult.

Inside Iran, inflation is running high and the value of the toman has fallen catastrophically against the pound. The sanctions regime is producing severe shortages of vital medicines and other necessary goods. Pollution is often so bad in Tehran that schools have to close. One of Iran's responses, beyond threatening to close the Straits of Hormuz, has been to say in autumn 2012 that it will no longer recognize British university degrees, which has thrown the many Iranians studying in Britain into a panic.

A new tactic, previously unknown in international politics, which the Islamic Republic used to put pressure on BBC PTV, was to threaten and harass family and friends of BBC PTV's employees inside Iran. For example, in the summer of 2012 a couple of young Iranian women were arrested and accused of collaborating with BBC PTV. Ironically, one of them, Parastoo Dokouhaki, had completed her postgraduate studies in London and had been one of the few to resist the hard currency salary of the BBC to return to Iran to work. A rapid campaign by her London-based friends, arguing that massive publicity was one of the only tools left to embarrass the regime, helped gain her fairly quick release – but this was another example of the paranoia about BBC PTV that the regime had engendered. Through the autumn of 2012 and in early 2013 there had been an escalating campaign against the BBC. Many employees in London had their family members in Iran questioned or detained as the regime tried to use family pressure to frighten the London-based employees; others had to withstand regime-generated rumours about their personal lives.

In the run up to the June 2013 election, this campaign escalated to include death threats against some BBC employees. In a statement issued by Liliane Landor, the Controller for Languages Services at the World Service, about the intimidation of BBC Persian staff and their families, she wrote:

> In the past few days alone, 15 family members have been summoned for questioning by the Intelligence Ministry in Tehran and in other cities across the country. The harassment has included threats that relatives will lose jobs and pensions and be prevented from travelling abroad. For the first time the lives of BBC Persian TV staff living in the UK have also been threatened.[64]

She continued by noting that audiences inside Iran for BBC PTV had reached 11.8 million, a recognition of 'the professionalism and resilience of our journalists, and to the value of their work delivering unbiased news and programmes to Persian-speaking audiences'.

If the 2009 election was the fiery baptism of BBC PTV, the 2013 presidential election showed its coming of age. Still unable to function inside Iran and under increasingly hostile rhetoric, the BBC PTV team developed plans for the best coverage they could provide under the circumstances. A mix of broadcasting and online activities has been a feature of BBC PTV activity from the beginning; the service has an online editor as well as a broadcasting editor. For example, its innovative programme *Nobat-e Shoma* (*Your Turn*) usually sets a topic for discussion and invites participation from Iranians at home and in the diaspora, effected through phone calls where possible, emails and text messages; a special social media team is trained to vet calls, ensure safety and anonymity if desired, and produce a lively programme.

The election was scheduled for 14 June.[65] Five months in advance, a special election editor, Mehdi Parpanchi, was appointed to oversee all BBC PTV election coverage. By 60 days before the election, the online team had developed two web pages dedicated to it. One was purely informational, with details of the process, the candidates and historical background. The second was a live page, moderated, that included external links, user-generated content and comments. These pages quickly found a viewership.

The typical idea of a road trip to cover the election was clearly out of the question, Iran being off-limits; but equally, given regime hostilities, few people in the diaspora were keen to talk on camera. The Islamic Republic's actions were having a muzzling effect. Town-hall meetings with lively debates were held and filmed in Istanbul – where a large Iranian refugee population lives in limbo – and Toronto. They were each half an hour long and had four guests from the Iranian diaspora. In Istanbul two were recent arrivals, while the Toronto guests were from established communities with interesting things to say about changing perceptions of Iranians, as Iran got more and more negative publicity under Ahmadinejad. Plans for events in Paris and Frankfurt were scuppered by an aeroplane over-running at Heathrow, which closed the airport.

Fifty different short packages were prepared for insertion into the nightly *60 Minutes* review programme and the twice-daily news bulletins; a selection of the best was re-versioned for English. Topics included a look at the way Iran has changed under the Ahmadinejad administration, touching on foreign policy, women, culture and sport. Taxi-driver 'postcards' were a way to ask how views of Iran have changed under Ahmadinejad, using the time-honoured journalistic method of talking to local cabbies in the Arab world, the US and the UK – in each case nationals of each country, not Iranians. Some Iranian celebrities and various Iran experts also made such shorts. One of the hardest tasks remained trying to include regime voices. Farhad Jafari, an outspoken supporter of Ahmadinejad, travelled to Turkey to record a lengthy interview; but few others would cooperate. And a number of films were produced, including an overview of Ahmadinejad's presidency. This was produced in both Persian and English versions, the latter shown at a Frontline Club gathering of foreign journalists. Programmes are live-streamed on the BBC Persian website. Additionally, recorded audio-visual materials were posted on the BBC website and, to avoid jamming, on YouTube.

Talks with BBC PTV journalists in the week before the election revealed that they were at pains to insist that they were not in the business of encouraging people to vote (or, indeed, not to vote) and that they were simply following the process, not leading it. 'Whatever we do is based on facts, with BBC quality our main concern', said Mehdi Parpanchi.[66]

And while not directly part of the Persian story, it is worth noting that the general move of BBC news-gathering operations to the shiny New Broadcasting House in central London has brought all the language services into far greater proximity with each other and with English-language news production. Daily meetings of all the services allow them to share breaking news stories, and bilingual journalists from the language services are called on to report and comment in English on stories from their country or region.

For the election, BBC Persian offered five bilingual Persian journalists who reported in English for global audiences as well as in Persian for BBC PTV: Rana Rahimpour, Amir Paivar, Kasra Naji, Pooneh Ghoddoosi as well as Saeed Barzin, who was hired as a consultant on a short-term basis to be their in-house analyst. For the days just before the election, someone from BBC PTV was based inside the English newsroom, providing a link to the materials coming in to BBC PTV from Iran and advice and interpretation as to their meaning. These are exciting innovations in journalistic practice, but it remains to be seen what impact these make on the range and depth of news coverage over the long term. Certainly, for BBC PTV journalists themselves, there is a greater sense of integration into the wider BBC: 'I bump into Andrew Marr in the corridor and think, wow, this *is* where I work!' said one BBC PTV female journalist.[67] Perhaps also there is a feeling that they are getting the recognition they deserve; in late May, the news team were delighted to have won an internal BBC award for their television news coverage.

The 2013 election process started timidly but burst into life in the final week, when only six of the eight approved candidates remained; the only clerical figure, Hassan Rouhani, with a law degree from a Scottish university and experience of nuclear negotiations, garnered the support of ex-presidents Khatami and Rafsanjani to become the unlikely reformist candidate. Gradually the '*Begoo nah!*' (Say No!) and the 'Vote for Zahra' (a cartoon female) social media campaigns gave way to people persuading others to vote since change was once more in the air. On election night the BBC PTV crew were on air for a marathon 25.5 hours, bringing live coverage of the election count with interviews and expert commentators in the studio, discussion and user-generated content. BBC PTV received hundreds of text messages from people in Iran begging them not to go off air as Iranians were enthralled by another nail-biting political moment. IRIB had given up covering the election at around 2 o'clock on Saturday morning, and started showing a film about zombies.[68]

The shift in mood produced an astonishing win for Rouhani at the first ballot. He called this 'the victory of moderation over extremism'. His subsequent tweets and statements have focused on many topics, including sanctions and nuclear negotiations as well as the media, internet and censorship. He seems to recognize both that IRIB has lost valuable audiences to external broadcasting channels that have offered a far higher standard of news production and entertainment, and that internet censorship has proved to be nigh-on impossible and pointless. In a live broadcast of an IRIB conference on 29 June, he suggested that IRIB needed to win back popular trust and discussed the need for a more open media environment, saying: 'The age of monologue media is over; media should be interactive [...] In a country whose legitimacy is rooted in its people, then there is no fear from free media.'[69] Further, in a public speech in early July, he asked rhetorically: 'Which important piece of news has filtering been able to black out in recent years?'[70]

BBC PTV remains one of the few ways for Britain and Iran to 'communicate' and for Iranians to hear something more balanced about the outside world. While formal international diplomacy has seemed to fail with Iran, it appears that the cultural diplomacy of media and artistic outreach and the public diplomacy embodied by the BBC world services become ever more significant. The indications are that the incoming president understands the nature of contemporary international communication rather better than his predecessor and realizes that keeping Iran in isolation and incommunicado does not help. How fast he is able to make real change, and what the implications for BBC PTV might be, remain key questions for Iran-watchers.

Conclusion

This volume does not provide a history of Iran, nor indeed even a history of Anglo–Iranian relations. But in our focus on the role of the BBC World Service in Afghanistan and Iran, we have – inevitably – had to reprise large chunks of Iran's modern history to show the significant and complex role that the Service has played in mediating relations. It was important to illustrate how and why the tension between Iran and Britain rose, often to crisis point, in four crucial periods – Reza Shah's abdication, Mossadeq's oil nationalization, the Iranian Revolution and the recent post-presidential election protests of 2009 – and how during these periods the BBC broadcasting in Persian found itself at the centre of a political tug of war. We have also tried to illustrate the nuances in the history of relations between the FCO and the BBC Persian Service and how these – contrary to general belief – have never been pre-defined or rigid; indeed, how both institutions have moved from an interest in what can crudely be called state-orchestrated 'propaganda' to a more subtle advocacy of fair and balanced journalism as the best agent of British values and influence.

In relation to Iran, in all the critical periods we examined, the BBC Persian Service was regarded with both suspicion and admiration by both the government of the day and the opposition. Rather ironically, it was severely criticized by the Shah for being pro-revolution in 1979 and then criticized by the Islamic Republic for being pro-West, indeed of even fomenting a 'soft topple' of the Islamic Republic, in 2009 – as if Iranians needed an outside voice to prompt them to act. All Iranian leaders of the period under analysis (Reza Pahlavi, Mohammad Reza Pahlavi, Khomeini, Khamenei) listened to the BBC Persian Service and took it seriously. Often they felt it was good to listen to it to hear the 'British point of view'. Others saw it not so much as presenting a British position so much as clear facts and analysis of the news story.

In Afghanistan too, both the Taliban and the Mujahedin criticized the BBC broadcasts to Afghanistan during the 1990s while they all listened religiously to keep up to date with their own civil war.

National memory is an important phenomenon in the period we cover. The memory of historical British meddling in Iran was very much linked to the BBC Persian Service from the time of Reza Shah's abdication, to the period of oil nationalization and the coup of 1953. It remains within the collective memory of Persians, was exacerbated by the dynamics of 1978–9 and reverberated again in the collective psyche in 2009. There is no surprise when these old sensitivities are sharpened at every crisis moment. Probably little that we have written here will discourage those who remain convinced that the BBC Persian Service is nothing but a mouthpiece of the British government. What we have tried to show is the struggle between the FO/FCO and the BBC World Service from the start. While BBC World Service content may, at times, have echoed British government positions, this is *not* necessarily because of direct FCO intervention to produce state propaganda. Our work did not include an analysis of BBC World Service content at these crucial moments, a huge research task that we leave for others.

We have argued that the BBC World Service is inevitably permeated with a British point of view, British values. Every media channel will in some way reflect its national origins, a kind of cultural unconscious that works to determine the agenda, framing and content of all media output. But that is *not* the same thing as being the mouthpiece of a state or following the instructions of the FCO. We clearly saw the contention between the BBC Persian Service and the FCO in relation to the Iranian Revolution of 1979 and we have seen a very different relationship between the organizations evolve during the 70 or so years of this story.

It is evident that the BBC World Service and its various language services have changed greatly in the manner in which they handled news reporting and in their relations with the Foreign Office. To begin with, the language services and the foreign nationals they employed were essentially 'readers' of translations of English-language news stories produced by central news. From the 1970s this pattern changed, as did the influence of the Foreign Office. In the 1980s the practices of the BBC home services were brought to the BBC World Service with extensive training courses provided in journalism and with the extension of the BBC's Producer Guidelines which advocate accuracy, objectivity and impartiality. By 2011, the LOTE services were run by teams of nationals or native language speakers far more in tune with the subtleties and complexities of events in their own countries and with full editorial control over their own content. If there is any serious charge of 'bias' to be levelled at the BBC Persian Service, it is that in all periods, but especially during 1978–9 and after June 2009, the Persian staff have told us that they were on the side of democratization – not necessarily on the side of the British. And democracy is not a bad side to favour!

We have also argued that the relationship between the FCO and the BBC Persian Service has never been black and white. Much depends on the circumstances and on who happens to be in charge in both. The BBC Charter is generally respected and there is always an implied understanding of the role of the BBC in being at the service of the public. We saw in the early chapters how initially the Foreign Office directly influenced the BBC but that later this equation changed. Despite the fact that the Shah was seen by the FCO as being the most loyal friend of Britain, his calls in 1978–9 for blocking the BBC Persian Service broadcasts went unheeded. In fact, there was little the FCO could do to influence the BBC reporting of an unfolding revolution.

From the late 1970s the FCO was gradually pushed back. We have shown how, during the year leading up to the Iranian Revolution, the BBC's Mark Dodd was able to push back constant pressure and unreasonable criticism from the British ambassador in Tehran, Anthony Parsons, and how in turn the Foreign Secretary, David Owen, was determined that there should be little interference with the work of the BBC. In practice, the FCO increasingly realized that the BBC would be more effective around the world if trusted by the listeners as being independent. The BBC World Service now has 'an understanding' about the government's international strategy and functions under the rubric of 'public diplomacy'.

Yet we have shown another variation too in the chapter on broadcasts to Afghanistan. Here the FCO saw in the BBC Persian Service a unique mechanism to access almost 80 per cent of the population in a country that Britain, together with her allies, had invaded following the 9/11 attack on the US. Suddenly high-level politicians such as the then Prime Minister Tony Blair or the then US Vice-President Dick Chaney became 'available for interviews'. More recently the US President Barack Obama, the Secretary of State Hillary Clinton, the British Foreign Secretary William Hague and several other high-ranking military and civilian officials have given interviews to the BBC PTV as a means of communicating with Iranians or Afghans. These types of 'request' interviews, which seem to be happening with more frequency, indicate a new form of cooperation between the FCO and the BBC. It seems they benefit both: BBC Persian Service gets interview 'scoops' and 'exclusives', and the FCO and its allies communicate their political message through a medium that has authority and the highest number of viewers. Yet it must be remembered that BBC editors and journalists can easily reject such official interview requests since they alone have the final say in all decisions on programming.

BBC Persian Service (radio, television and web) is operating in an increasingly competitive market. On the world stage it has to compete with similar brands produced in the US (VOA and

RFE/RL), Russia (VOR), Germany (Deutsche Welle), EU (Euronews Persian TV and web page), Israel, Japan and China (China Radio International). Yet it has to distinguish itself by upholding its BBC brand through balanced reporting of the news. It may or may not succeed in that, but that is the only way it can stay ahead of its rivals. While some prefer to see it as part of the establishment, the BBC has had no choice but to keep its capacity to speak factually and truthfully.

It is precisely because the BBC has had the ability to lead the market that the FCO tries to approach it at times of crisis and make funds available for more programming. We saw how, for example, the FCO had no interest in setting up a Pashto Service until the Soviet invasion of Afghanistan in 1980. We also saw how after 9/11 the BBC request for setting up a daily three-hour slot was accepted and then later BBC for Afghanistan was set up with far wider coverage. We also saw that despite a period of austerity for the BBC, the FCO supported the move into television, at first in Arabic, and subsequently provided an annual budget of £15 million for setting up an eight-hour daily television broadcast for Iran and Afghanistan. Certainly through this funding mechanism, the FCO has had the possibility to encourage or discourage BBC programming to different parts of the world, and to accept or reject BBC language service bids for funding to ensure it gets best value for its international priorities and zones of influence.

Yet, inside the FCO there has been an ongoing debate about the value of the BBC, how, when and where it should be approached. We saw in Chapter 3 – the last period for which we have firsthand FCO documents – that there was disagreement and debate amongst FCO officials and analysts over what constitutes 'national interest', and whether it is the short-term or long-term British national interests that should matter most when it comes to political communication. So, again, these nuances of public diplomacy are not rigid and are subject to variations.

However, a major change to this historic relationship is in the offing. In October 2010, as part of the broad Coalition government spending review, major changes were announced.

Not only would the BBC in general face cuts of 16 per cent, which has already resulted in numerous redundancies; more significant still was the decision that the BBC will take on responsibility for funding the World Service. The BBC would also be financially responsible for BBC Monitoring, and part-funding S4C, as well as helping to meet the cost of rolling out broadband internet access to rural areas. All of which is estimated to save the government £340 million from general taxation, requiring annual savings of £46 million. In April 2014, the FCO grant-in-aid funding will come to an end and the BBC World Service transfers to television licence fee funding.

To achieve the savings, the director of the BBC World Service, Peter Horrocks, announced the complete closure of five language services – Albanian, Macedonian, Portuguese for Africa and Serbian languages, as well as the English for the Caribbean regional service. All radio programming would end in Azeri, Mandarin Chinese, Russian, Spanish for Cuba, Turkish, Vietnamese and Ukrainian, with a move instead to online, mobile and television content and distribution for these services. There will also be a phased reduction in medium-wave and shortwave throughout the period. There is already a commercially driven platform for the US, and suggestions of the introduction of advertising elsewhere. There is a move to more platform-sharing with international broadcasters – as in Turkey – with the BBC World Service keeping tight editorial control over content. And expansions are not ruled out, with proposals for a television channel in Urdu.

So as has been the pattern throughout the 75-plus years of the World Service, countries deemed on the path to 'democracy' are no longer felt to require a language service while online and television audiences are deemed to be the future, over loyal radio audiences. The consolidation of news production in one building and the rebranding as BBC World indicate that not only the BBC World Service funding structure but its entire ethos looks set to change quite radically. The text on the website declares:

Welcome to BBC Broadcasting House, the new state of the art, multimedia broadcasting centre in the heart of London. This world-class facility is the iconic new home for the BBC's network and global services in Television, Radio, News and Online. Delivering the vision of 'One BBC', new Broadcasting House heralds a simpler, more integrated digital service for audiences, and a simpler, more creative environment for staff. The redesign will save the BBC £736m over a 20-year period.[1]

With the move to direct public funding through the licence fee, it will be fascinating to see whether a new narrative about the BBC's international role emerges, and whether British audiences appreciate the need for and benefits of such expenditure on external audiences.[2]

For Iran, it is evident that first the BBC radio service and now the combined platforms of radio, television and online have been significant sources of news, often at times when the domestic channels did not trust the population with the relevant information. There is a sizeable audience inside Iran for BBC PTV, around 12 million people, which has by its very existence revealed the weakness and limitations of broadcasting from the Islamic Republic. Indeed, there are indications that IRIB channels altered their look and their logo in a backhanded compliment to BBC PTV. For Iranians, it is to be hoped that President Rouhani will open up the Iranian media environment so that BBC PTV becomes just another useful media channel in a cacophony of competitors. Then it will really have made a difference!

The future holds a lot of questions: about Anglo–Iranian relations, the nature of the Iranian political system and the internal struggle to protect free and independent media, and the struggle of the BBC World Service, especially its LOTE channels, to maintain a worldwide 'public service' in highly competitive times. There are many challenges ahead.

We wish all those on the side of free speech and democracy well, wherever they are.

Notes

Introduction: The BBC World Service and Iran: 70 Years of the Delicate Dance

1   Reporters Without Borders, *Press Freedom Index 2013*. Available at http://en.rsf.org/press-freedom-index-2013,1054.html (accessed 5 July 2013).

2   The concept of 'soft power' will be discussed in Chapter 1.

3   The Foreign Office (FO) became the Foreign and Commonwealth Office (FCO) in 1968. Throughout the book we try to use the coinage of the period in question.

4   *The War of Words*, the third volume of Asa Brigg's *History of Broadcasting in the United Kingdom* (Oxford, 1995), is about the propaganda battle between Britain and Germany, which led to the creation of foreign-language broadcasting by the BBC. There's also Andrew Walker's 1992 book, *A Skyful of Freedom: 60 Years of the BBC World Service* (London, 1992), a history published by the World Service itself.

5   'Tuning In: BBC World Service' was an AHRC-funded project led by Professor Marie Gillespie of the Open University, with six focal strands, giving a new impetus to research on the World Service. Annabelle Sreberny was the primary investigator on the strand of the project called 'diasporic nationalism'. See www.open.ac.uk/

researchprojects/diasporas/core-research/diasporic-nationhood for more information (accessed 7 June 2013).

6   Massoumeh Torfeh also incorporated some of the documents of the US State Department that she had collected during the 1990s when she was conducting her doctoral research on 'The Causes of the Failure of Democracy in Iran' at the London School of Economics and Political Science.

7   The Foreign Office references sometimes include the recipient, but not always, and usually include the author and date. Occasionally there is only a reference number. The references are presented as listed in the archives, and can always be located with the reference number.

8   See www.soas.ac.uk/centresoffice/events/witness-seminar-iran for more information (accessed 7 June 2013).

Chapter 1: From Propaganda to Public Diplomacy: The Changing Paradigms

1   The source of this widely reported quotation is probably Reith's address to a select committee of MPs in which he said: 'I will not give the public what it wants or what it is supposed to want, if it knows what it wants. I will give it something much better than that. It will take it, and come back for more' (Simon Elmes, *Hello Again: Nine Decades of Radio Voices* (London, 2013), p. 45).

2   From the BBC World Service's audio archive; see www.bbc.co.uk/worldservice/specials/1122_75_years (accessed 5 July 2013).

3   In celebration of the 80th anniversary of the World Service, considerable materials including early broadcasts were made available on the BBC website: www.bbc.co.uk/historyofthebbc/great_moments/index.shtml (accessed 28 June 2013).

4   BBC World Service, *75 Years: BBC World Service: A History* (2007). Available at www.bbc.co.uk/worldservice/history/timeline.shtml (accessed 28 June 2013).

5   Peter Partner, *Arab Voices: The BBC Arabic Service 1938–1988* (London, 1988), p. 38.

6   Fatima El Issawi and Gerd Baumann, 'The BBC Arabic Service: changing political mediascapes', *Middle East Journal of Culture and Communication* 3/2, pp. 137–51.

7   BBC Trust, *BBC Public Purpose Remit: Bringing the UK to the World and the World to the UK* (London, 2007), p. 1. Available at www.bbc.co.uk/bbctrust/assets/files/pdf/about/how_we_govern/ purpose_remits/bringing.pdf (accessed 28 June 2013).

8   Sir Michael Lyons, Chairman of the BBC Trust, 'Public value and the BBC's international role', speech to Sweden's Public Service Day (2011). Available at www.bbc.co.uk/bbctrust/news/ speeches/2011/global_mission.html (accessed 28 June 2013).

9   University of Southern California Center on Public Diplomacy, 'What is public diplomacy?' Available at http://uscpublicdiplomacy.org/index.php/about/what_is_pd (accessed 28 June 2013).

10   Hans N. Tuch, *Communicating with the World: US Public Diplomacy Overseas* (New York, 1990), p. 3.

11   Hady Amr, *The Need to Communicate: How to Improve US Public Diplomacy with the Islamic World* (Washington, DC, 2004).

12   James Pamment, *New Public Diplomacy in the 21st Century* (Abingdon and New York, 2012), p. 20.

13   Jian Wang and Tsan-Kuo Chang, 'Strategic public diplomacy and local press: How a high profile "head-of-state" visit was covered in America's heartland', *Public Relations Review* 30 (2004), pp. 11–24.

14   General Accounting Office (GAO), 'US international broadcasting: New strategic approach focuses on reaching large audiences but lacks measurable program objectives' (Report to the Committee on International Relations, House of Representatives, GAO-03-951) (Washington, DC, 2003).

15   Ibid. See also Mohan Dutta-Bergman, 'U.S. Public Diplomacy in the Middle East: A Critical Cultural Approach', *Journal of Communication Inquiry* 30/2 (2006), pp. 102–24.

16   Joseph Nye, *Soft Power: The Means to Success in World Politics* (New York, 2004).

17   Herb Schiller, 'Not yet the Post-Imperial Era', *Critical Studies in Mass Communication* 8/1.

18   Joseph Nye, 'The new public diplomacy', *Project Syndicate* (2010). Available at www.project-syndicate.org/commentary/the-new-public-diplomacy (accessed 5 July 2013).

19   Ibid.

20   Richard L. Armitage and Joseph S. Nye, Jr, *CSIS Commission on Smart Power: A Smarter, More Secure America* (Washington, DC, 2007), p. 7.

21 Nye, 'The new public diplomacy'.

22 Mark Leonard, Catherine Stead and Conrad Smewing, *Public Diplomacy* (London, 2002), p. 6.

23 Ibid., p. 7.

24 Select Committee on Foreign Affairs, Third Report: 2. Public Diplomacy (2006). Available at www.publications.parliament.uk/pa/cm200506/cmselect/cmfaff/903/90305.htm (accessed 5 July 2013).

25 Lord Carter of Coles, *Review of Public Diplomacy* (London, 2005), p. 71, Annex F, para i.

26 Mark Leonard and Andrew Small with Martin Rose, *British Public Diplomacy in the 'Age of Schisms'* (London, 2005), pp. 36–7.

27 *Government Response to the Foreign Affairs Committee Report on Public Diplomacy*, Cm 6840, June 2006.

28 Ibid.

29 Foreign Affairs Committee, Fifth Report of Session 2009–10, *Foreign and Commonwealth Office Annual Report 2008–09*, HC 145, paras 285, 287.

30 Rt Hon William Hague, 'Britain's foreign policy in a networked world', speech at FCO, 1 July 2010. Available at www.conservatives.com/News/Speeches/2010/07/William_Hague_Britains_Foreign_Policy_in_a_Networked_World.aspx (accessed 5 July 2013).

31 As of September 2013, there is a House of Lords ad hoc committee working on 'soft power and the UK's infuence'. See http://bit.ly/16Snxnr for more information.

32 Foreign and Commonwealth Office, Westminster Hall debate: Effects on diplomacy of internet technologies, 22 December 2010. Available at www.gov.uk/government/speeches/westminster-hall-debate-effects-on-diplomacy-of-internet-technologies (accessed 5 July 2013).

33 Matilda Anderson, Marie Gillespie and Hugh Mackay, 'Mapping digital diasporas @ BBC World Service: users and uses of the Persian and Arabic websites', *Middle East Journal of Culture and Communication* 3/2 (2013), pp. 256–78.

34 BBC press release, 'BBC World Service cuts language services and radio broadcasts to meet tough Spending Review settlement', 26 January 2011. Available at www.bbc.co.uk/pressoffice/pressreleases/stories/2011/01_january/26/worldservice.shtml (accessed 5 July 2013).

35 Over the summer of 2013, there has been a 'Public Consultation on BBC Trust governance of BBC World Service, via an operating licence'. Available at www.bbc.co.uk/bbctrust/have_your_say/world_service.html (accessed 9 October 2013). It remains to be seen what recommendations emerge.

36 Nima Adelkhah, 'Iran integrates the concept of "soft war" into its strategic planning', *Jamestown Foundation Terrorism Monitor* 8/23 (2010). Available at www.jamestown.org/programs/tm/archivesgta/2010 (accessed 5 July 2013).

37 Samuel P. Huntington, 'The Clash of Civilizations?', *Foreign Affairs* 72/3 (1993), pp. 22–49.

38 Adelkhah, 'Iran integrates the concept of "soft war" into its strategic planning'.

39 Hamid Mowlana, cited in Maaike Warnaar, *So Many Similarities: Linking Domestic Dissent to Foreign Threat in Iran*. Working Paper No. 20, Knowledge Programme Civil Society in West Asia, HIVOS and Amsterdam Institute for Social Science Research (AISSR), University of Amsterdam (2011).

40 IRNA news agency, Tehran (0639 GMT, 26 April 2007), in Persian; translation by BBC Monitoring, accessed through http://bbcmonitoringlibrary.com.ezproxy.soas.ac.uk/bbcm (accessed December 2012).

41 IRNA website, Tehran (1940 GMT, 9 June 2007), in English; trans-lation by BBC Monitoring, accessed through http://bbcmonitoringlibrary.com.ezproxy.soas.ac.uk/bbcm (accessed December 2012).

42 Hamid Omidi, 'The arena of two rivals', *Keyhan* website, Tehran (22 February 2009), in Persian; translation by BBC Monitoring: '"Soft war" against Iran to be speedier under Democrats' (24 February 2009). Available at www.accessmylibrary.com/coms2/summary_0286-36838514_ITM (accessed 5 July 2013).

43 See Biyokulule Online: 'Iran paper says cultural NATO more dangerous than military one' (21 August 2007), which gives text of report headlined 'The supreme jurisconsult's representative in Revolution Guards' Corps: NATO's cultural function is considerably more dangerous than its military one', published by Iranian newspaper Kayhan website, Tehran, on 19 August 2007, in Persian. Available at www.biyokulule.com/view_content.php?articleid=402 (accessed 5 July 2013).

44   That there are clear parallels of argument in the West is evident. We note just one sentence from a recent article by Retired Maj. Gen. Robert H. Scales, former US Army War College commander and deputy chief of staff for doctrine: 'To win World War IV, the military must be culturally knowledgeable enough to thrive in an alien environment. Victory will be defined more in terms of capturing the psycho-cultural rather than the geographical high ground. Understanding and empathy will be important weapons of war.' Maj. Gen. Robert H. Scales, 'Clausewitz and World War IV', *Armed Forces Journal* (July 2006). Available at www.armedforcesjournal.com/2006/07/1866019 (accessed 5 July 2013).

45   Ali Shirin, 'The media are the main instruments of soft power and soft threat' (Interview with Ali Mohammad Na'ini), *Javan*, 26 November 2009.

46   Ibid.

47   *Huffington Post*, '"Soft war" on Iran is biggest threat to country, Gen. Mohammad Ali Jafari claims', 3 August 2012. Available at www.huffingtonpost.com/2012/08/03/soft-war-iran_n_1739448.html (accessed 6 July 2013).

48   Ibid.

49   *Resalat*, Tehran (15 September 2009), in Persian, p. 2; translation by BBC Monitoring, accessed through http://bbcmonitoringlibrary.com.ezproxy.soas.ac.uk/bbcm (accessed December 2012).

50   Available in Persian at http://alef.ir.

51   See Warnaar, *So Many Similarities*; Adelkhah, 'Iran integrates the concept of "soft war" into its strategic planning'. See also Annabelle Sreberny, 'Too soft on "soft war": Commentary on Monroe Price's "Iran and the Soft War"', *International Journal of Communication* 7 (2013), Feature 801–4. Available at http://eprints.soas.ac.uk/15696/1/AS%20IoJC%202004-8001-1-PB.pdf (accessed 11 September 2013).

Chapter 2: The Establishment of BBC World Service Persian Radio

1   See Denis Wright, *The English Amongst the Persians* (London, 1977); and *The Persians Amongst the English* (London, 1985).

Notes **183**

2   Stephen Kinzer, *All the Shah's Men: An American Coup and the Roots of Middle East Terror* (Princeton, NJ, 2008).

3   Maryam Borjian, 'The rise and fall of a partnership: The British Council and the Islamic Republic of Iran (2001–09)', *Iranian Studies* 44/4 (2011), pp. 541–62.

4   Abbas Milani, *The Shah* (New York, 2011), p. 60.

5   Foreign Office (FO) 371-24570/E587/2/34: Prepared by Press Attaché sent by H.J. Seymour. *The Persian Press*, 20 September 1939.

6   FO371-24570/EP 2011/15: From British Embassy in Tehran to Foreign Office. Telegram No. 144, 1 October 1939.

7   FO371-24570: From Baggallay at the Foreign Office to Sir Reader Bullard, 8 February 1940.

8   FO371-24570: The Foreign Office to Tehran, 16 February 1940.

9   Ibid.

10 FO371-24570/E1870/2/34: From Sir Reader Bullard in the British Legation in Tehran to R.S. Stevenson at the Foreign Office, 5 June 1940.

11 Hedayat Matin-Daftari, interview with Massoumeh Torfeh, Paris, 29 July 2010.

12 Ibid.

13 FO371-27185/E7767/211/34: From Sir Reader Bullard to Foreign Office, 22 November 1941.

14 FO371-27185/E7767/211/34: From Sir Reader Bullard to Foreign Office, 22 November 1941.

15 FO371-24570/E2/2/34: From Lacey Baggallay at the Foreign Office to Sir Reader Bullar, 8 February 1940.

16 Ibid.

17 FO371-24570/E1484: 2 April 1940.

18 FO 371-24570/E842/2/34: From Coverly Price in FO to Ministry of Information, 13 June 1940.

19 FO371-24570, From Anne Lambton to Professor Rushbrook Williams, Ministry of Information, 21 December 1939.

20 Ibid.

21 FO371-24570/E2426: From the Foreign Office to the British Legation in Tehran, 16 August 1940.

22 Ibid.

23 Ibid.

24 Ibid.

25   Ibid.

26   FO371-24570: From Sir Reader Bullard to Foreign Secretary, 24 February 1940.

27   Ibid.

28   FO371-24570: From the Secretary of State to His Excellency Mohammad Ali Moghadam, 21 December 1940.

29   BBC Persian Service Archives, programme for the 65h anniversary produced by Shahryar Radpoor, an internally authorized account of the period.

30   Ibid.

31   FO371-28914: Foreign Office from A.W.Q. Randall to Mr Strange, 18 January 1941.

32   Ibid.

33   Ibid.

34   FO371-28914/W574: From Sir J. Anderson to Anthony Eden, *Propaganda in Enemy Countries in Enemy Occupation*, 10 January 1941.

35   Ibid.

36   Ibid.

37   FO371-27183/E211/211/34: Mr Elkington of the AIOC to C.W. Baxter, Foreign Office, 14 January 1941.

38   FO371-35089/E5035: Sir Anthony Eden writes to Sir Reader Bullard, 26 June 1941, saying that in a letter discovered by British Intelligence, Mayer was found to have written that the southern mountainous areas of Iran were a safe bastion for German military work, claiming that it 'is like a part of Germany or an unassailable allied state behind the enemy's lines in which you can do anything you wish, train, recruit and build landing ground, munitions dump and U-boat bases'.

39   FO371-35089/E5035: Sir Anthony Eden to Sir Reader Bullard, 26 June 1941.

40   FO371-35075/E5036: Mr. Hollman at the British Legation in Tehran to Foreign Office, 15 August 1943.

41   FO371-27183/E985/211/34: 12 March 1941.

42   FO371-27183/E382/211/34: From Sir Reader Bullard to the Foreign Office, *Nazi Propaganda*, 7 February 1941.

43   FO371-28914/34/211: Sir Reader Bullard. Most Secret, *Propaganda in Persia*, 7 August 1941.

44   Ibid.

45 FO371- 27184/4902/211/34: Sir Reader Bullard to Foreign Office, 22 August 1941.
46 Ibid.
47 FO371-27213/EP5518: Anthony Eden to British Legation in Teheran, 9 September 1941.
48 FO371-27183/E4028/211/34.
49 Ervand Abrahamian, *Iran Between Two Revolutions* (Princeton, NJ, 1982), p. 65.
50 FO371-35117/E239/34: Sir Reader Bullard to the Foreign Office, *Annual Report for the Year 1942*.
51 BBC Persian Service Archives, programme for the 65th anniversary of the BBC Persian Service, produced by Shahryar Radpoor.
52 BBC website, 'About BBC News: history: 1930s'. Available at http://news.bbc.co.uk/aboutbbcnews/spl/hi/history/html/1930s.stm (accessed 27 June 2013).
53 Hossein Shahidi, 'BBC Persian Service – 60 years on', *The Iranian* (web page), 24 September 2001. Available at http://iranian.com/History/2001/September/BBC (accessed 27 June 2013).
54 BBC Persian Service Archives, programme for the 65th anniversary of the BBC Persian Service, produced by Shahryar Radpoor.
55 Ibid.
56 Abrahamian, *Iran*, p. 65.
57 Ibid.
58 Reader S. Bullard, *Britain and the Middle East*, Third Revised Edition (London, 1964), p. 135.
59 Cited in BBC WAC. E40/657/1: *Some Notes on the Origins and History of the Persian Service*.
60 Ibid.
61 FO371-35069/E1448-EE1574: Sir Reader Bullard to Sir Anthony Eden, March 1943.
62 FO371-35070/E2030: Sir Reader Bullard to Foreign Office. 6 April 1943.
63 FO371-35098/E2794: Sir Reader Bullard to Anthony Eden, 14 May 1943.
64 Ibid.
65 FO371-40194/E3248: Sir Reader Bullard to Foreign Office, 9 June 1944.
66 FO371-27153/E2081/38/34: Sir Reader Bullard to Foreign Office, 9 April 1943.

67   FO371/3201: The British Council in Iran.

68   FO371/40194/E3596: Sir Reader Bullard to all Councils in Iran, 20 June 1944.

69   FO371-24570: From Anne Lambton to Professor Rushbrook Williams, Ministry of Information, 21 December 1939.

70   Ibid.

71   Foreign Service of the United States of America, communication from American Embassy, Tehran, to Department of State, Washington, DC, 12 January 1951. Ref. XR 511.884.

72   Ibid.

73   Mohan Dutta-Bergman, 'U.S. public diplomacy in the Middle East: A critical cultural approach', *Journal of Communication Inquiry* 30/2 (2006), pp. 102–24.

74   Operations Coordinating Board, 'Detailed development of actions relating to the Near East' (Washington, DC, 1955).

Chapter 3: The BBC World Service, the British Government and the Nationalization of Iranian Oil

1   Mohammad Mossadeq, *The Proceedings of the Fourteenth Majlis: Session 13*, 5 March 1944. The Archives of the Iranian Parliament, Tehran.

2   Cited in Stephen Kinzer, *All the Shah's Men: An American Coup and the Roots of Middle East Terror* (Princeton, NJ, 2008), p. 68.

3   Ibid.

4   FO37140194/E3596: Sir Reader Bullard to all Councils in Iran, 20 June 1944.

5   BBC World Service website: 'History: The 1930s'. Available at www.bbc.co.uk/worldservice/history/story/2007/02/070123_html_1930s.shtml (accessed 27 June 2013).

6   FCO 8/3212: Review of the BBC Persian Service, H.H.E. Lancashire, 9 November 1977.

7   BBC World Service website: 'History: The 1940s'. Available at www.bbc.co.uk/worldservice/history/story/2007/02/070122_html_40s.shtml (accessed 27 June 2013).

8   FO371/68708-236: Confidential. From Foreign Office to Tehran, No. 702, 6 November 1948.

9   FO371/68708-236: Secret. From Foreign Office to Tehran, No. 704, 6 November 1948.

10   FO371/68708-236: Secret. From Foreign Office to Tehran, No. 707, 7 November 1948.

11   FO371/75467-1333443: From Tehran to Foreign Office, 9 November 1949.

12   FO371/75467-1333443: Political Situation in Persia, 19 November 1949.

13   Ibid.

14   Kinzer, *All the Shah's Men*.

15   FO371/8231/EP1016/27: From the British Embassy in Tehran to the Foreign Secretary, Ernest Bevin, 7 April 1950.

16   Kinzer, *All the Shah's Men*, p. 75.

17   FO371/82310: From Sir Francis Shepherd to The Right Honorable Ernest Bevin, HM Principal Secretary of State for Foreign Affairs, 7 April 1950.

18   Kinzer, *All the Shah's Men*, p. 76.

19   FO371/ 91448-565: Report on Events in Persia During 1950, December 1950.

20   FO371/82311: From Foreign Office to Tehran, 6 May 1950.

21   FO371/98593: Report on Events in Persia in 1951, December 1951.

22   FO371/91523: *Keshvar* newspaper, organ of the National Front, 16 February 1951.

23   FO371-91523/EP1531/68: From Sir Francis Shepherd in Tehran to FCO, 1 March 1951.

24   Ibid.

25   Ibid.

26   FO371-91523/EP1531/68: From Sir Francis Shepherd in Tehran to FCO, 1 March 1951.

27   Full text in FO371/91524/EP1531/122: 'Nationalization of oil', BBC Diplomatic Correspondent, 4 March 1951.

28   Ibid.

29   BBC Written Archives Centre (WAC): E40/657/1: 'Some notes on the origins and history of the BBC Persian Service.'

30   FO371/91453/565: *New York Times*, 8 August 1951.

31   FO371/91470/EP1023/21: From [the UK Embassy in] Washington to Foreign Office, Telegram No. 1098, 11 April 1951.

32   FO371/91470/EP1023/21: From [the UK Embassy in] Washington to Foreign Office, Telegram No. 1098, 11 April 1951.

33   FO371/91457/EP1015/168: Top-secret note on Persia, 21 April 1951.

34   FO371-91535/EP1531/358: BBC interview with Ahmad Maleki of *Setareh* newspaper, member of the National Front, 17 May 1951.

35   Ibid.

36   Mohammad Mossadeq, *The Proceedings of the Sixteenth Majlis*, Session 130, May 1951.

37   Mossadeq, *Sixteenth Majlis*, Session 130, May 1951.

38   F770003/2393: The US State Department, US National Archives. The Political Situation in Iran, January 1952, p. 29.

39   FO371/91460/699: Top Secret letter from the secretary of Chiefs of Staff Committee to the Ministry of Defence, 19 June 1951.

40   Ibid.

41   FO371/91460/699/EP1015/247: From Mr Furlong at FCO to Col. R.G.V. Fitzgeorge Balfour CBE, 26 June 1951.

42   As witnessed by Dr Massoumeh Torfeh, who was a senior producer in the BBC Persian Service 1986–98.

43   Yonah Alexander and Allan Nanes, *The United States and Iran, A Documentary History* (Maryland, 1980), p. 218.

44   Cited in Alexander and Nanes, *The United States and Iran*, p. 220.

45   Ibid., p. 222.

46   FO371/91472/699: From Tehran to Foreign Office. Mr Middleton, Telegram No. 1630, 7 November 1951.

47   Ibid.

48   FO371/98608/753/Ep1022/9: British Record of Meeting Held in the Foreign Office on 14 February 1952.

48   FO371/98593/753: Report on the Events in Persia in 1951.

50   Ibid.

51   Alexander and Nanes, *The United States and Iran*, p. 224.

52   Bahram Afrasiabi, *Mossadeq and History* (Tehran, 1979), p. 210.

53   FO371/98593/E753: From Sir J. Le Rougetel to the Foreign Office, December 1951.

54   Ibid.

55   Cited in FO371-91454/PRO.

56   FO371/ 98674: The British Point of View, September 1952.

57   Ibid.

58   F770003/2393: Unclassified Report of the US State Department. The Political Situation in Iran, January 1952.

59 BBC Persian Service Archives, programme for the 65th anniversary of the BBC Persian Service, produced by Shahryar Radpoor.

60 Ibid.

61 Hossein Shahidi, 'The BBC Persian Service, 1940–1953', *Journal of Iranian Research and Analysis* 17/1 (2001), p. 16.

62 Norman Kemp, *Abadan: A First-Hand Account of the Persian Oil Crisis* (London, 1953), p. 208.

63 Ibid., p. 146.

64 Cited in Kemp, *Abadan*, p. 198.

65 *Bakhtar Emruz*, British Library. Front Page, 15 January 1952.

66 Ibid.

67 *Bakhtar Emruz*, British Library. Front Page, 19 January 1952.

68 *Bakhtar Emruz*, British Library. Front Page, 28 January 1952.

69 Radio broadcast, January 1952. Available on Mardomak (website): www.mardomak.us/videos/full/50891.

70 The US State Department Documents, 89100/4-1352, 13 April 1952.

71 Ibid.

72 FO371/98608/EP1022/9: British Record of a Meeting held at the Foreign Office, 14 February 1952.

73 Ibid.

74 Kinzer, *All the Shah's Men*.

75 Ibid., p. 115.

76 FO371/98593/753: Report on the Events in Persia in 1951.

77 Mostafa Elm, *Oil, Power and Principle: Iran's Oil Nationalization and its Aftermath* (Syracuse, 1992).

78 FO371/98618/EP1051/21: George Middleton at the British Embassy to Archie D.M. Rose, Eastern Department, Foreign Office, 11 February 1952.

79 FO371/98599/753/EP1015/117: From Tehran to Foreign Office, 16 May 1952.

80 Elm, *Oil, Power and Principle*, p. 270.

81 FO371/104561: Political summary. Tehran, 22 December 1952.

82 Ibid.

83 FO371/104574/EP1017/1: Persian political summary December–January 1952–3.

84 FO371/104561: Political summary. Tehran, 22 December 1952.

85 See, for example, the US State Department 788-5 MAP/5-1751 or 788-8 MSP/1-352.

86   FO371/104574/EP1017/1: Persian political summary December–January 1952–3.

87   F770003-2373: Political Characteristics of Mossadeq. Central Intelligence Agency.

88   788.00/4-2153: The US State Department Secret Security Information, from Ambassador Loy Henderson in the US Embassy in Tehran. Estimate Tudeh Strengths and Activities, 21 April 1953.

89   FO371/98593/753: Report on the Events in Persia in 1951.

90   FO371/104561: Incoming Telegram from American Embassy in London, 5 January 1953.

91   Ibid.

92   FO371/104614/EP1531/228: Comment for Mossadeq Speech 11 December, 19 March 1953.

93   Laurence Paul Elwell-Sutton, *Persian Oil: A Study in Power Politics* (London, 1955), p. 241.

94   Ibid., p. 146.

95   *The Times*, 'Dr. Moussadek takes quick counter-attack', 2 March 1953.

96   Ibid.

97   FO371/104572/134399/EP1015/256: Political Events in Persia Since July 1953.

98   FO371/104659-134399: From Baghdad to Foreign Office, 17 August 1953.

99   Ibid.

100 FO371/194659/134399: From Washington to Foreign Office, 18 August 1953.

101 Ibid.

102 FO371/104659/134399: Account of an audience by the US ambassador Loy Henderson with the Shah, 6 June 1953.

103 Ibid.

104 FCO371/104564/EP1015/105: Top Secret from Washington to Foreign Office, Foreign Office secret and Whitehall secret distribution, 13 April 1953.

105 Ibid.

106 Abbas Milani, *The Shah* (New York, 2011), p. 171.

107 FO371/104571/134399: Summary of Political Developments in Iran 6–19 August 1953.

108 US State Department, Remarks by the Secretary of State Madeleine K. Albright on American–Iranian Relations, 17 March 2000.

Available at www.parstimes.com/history/albright_speech.html (accessed 27 June 2013). Further documents released in August 2013 show the involvement of the CIA with the British in the process of the coup. See Malcolm Byrne (ed.), 'CIA confirms role in 1953 Iran coup', 19 August 2013. Available at www2.gwu.edu/~nsarchiv/NSAEBB/NSAEBB435/#_ftn4 (accessed 21 August 2013).

109 Kermit Roosevelt, *Counter Coup: The Struggle for the Control of Iran* (New York, 1979).

110 Asadollah Alam, *The Shah and I* (London, 2008), p. 540.

111 Roosevelt, *Counter Coup*, p. 156.

112 See Milani, *The Shah*, p. 161; Kinzer, *All the Shah's Men*, pp. 9–10.

113 Al Jazeera, 'Iran's media: The new red lines', Listening Post episode, 2 February 2013. Available at www.aljazeera.com/programmes/listeningpost/2013/02/201321195034218716.html (accessed 11 September 2013).

114 Roosevelt, *Counter Coup*, p. 156.

115 FO371/104577/134273: 28 August 1953.

116 Ibid.

117 Ibid.

118 Mark Hollingsworth, 'Secrets and spies', *Guardian*, 8 April 2000. Available at www.guardian.co.uk/books/2000/apr/08/history.politics (accessed 27 June 2013).

119 FO371/104577/134273/EP1024/2: From the British Embassy in Washington to Foreign Office, 25 August 1953.

120 788.00/3-3154: Loy Henderson to the US Secretary of State, 18 March 1954.

121 88-56/11-3054: The US State Department, 30 November 1954.

122 FO371/104659/134399: Reply from Winston Churchill to the Shah of Persia. Nd (but clearly soon after the coup).

123 Dan De Luce, 'The spectre of Operation Ajax', *Guardian*, 20 August 2003. Available at www.guardian.co.uk/politics/2003/aug/20/foreignpolicy.iran (accessed 27 June 2013).

124 BBC WAC E40/657/1: 'Some notes on the origins and history of the Persian Service', p. 3.

Chapter 4: The BBC and the Iranian Revolution of 1979

1 Asadollah Alam, *The Shah and I* (London, 2008), p. 273.

2   Ibid., p. 357.

3   Ibid., p. 490.

4   There are several examples for this both in the documents of the Foreign Office when the Shah plays the Americans and the British against each other or against the Russians, and also in his conversations with his chief of protocol, Assadolah Alam. See Alam, *The Shah and I.*

5   Ibid., p. 535.

6   Ibid., p. 533.

7   Foreign and Commonwealth Office (FCO) 8/3212: Telegram from Sir Anthony Parsons, 15 December 1978, Public Records Office (PRO).

8   BBC Written Archives Center (BBC WAC). PB306/324/1: Review of the Persian Service. Copy of Telegram No. 425 from the British Ambassador in Tehran to the FCO, *The Financial Times* and the BBC Persian Service, 30 June 1976.

9   Ibid.

10   Ibid.

11   BBC WAC: Review of the Persian Service: Record of telephone conversation of Mark Dodd with N.J. Barrington, FCO, 1 July 1976.

12   Ibid.

13   FCO8/2762: Telegram from Anthony Parsons to Nicholas Barrington at FCO, 1 August 1976, PRO.

14   BBC WAC E58/25/1: Enclosure with letter from M.S. Buckmaster of FCO Guidance and Information Department to Mark Dodd at BBC, 11 April 1975.

15   Ibid.

16   BBC WAC E40/710/1: 15 July 1976.

17   FCO 8/2762: Telegram from Anthony Parsons to Nicholas Barrington at FCO, 1 August 1976, PRO.

18   BBC WAC E40/711/1: Confidential Minutes of BBC Board of Governors meeting, 8 July 1976.

19   BBC WAC E40/710/1: 15 July 1976.

20   Ibid.

21   Ibid.

22   FCO 8/3215: Text of the Licence and Agreement between the BBC and FCO, 7 July 1969.

23   BBC WAC E58/25/1: N.d. on document, suggested by WAC specialist to be between 11 and 28 April 1976.

24 Ibid.
25 Ibid.
26 Ibid.
27 FCO 8/2767: Telegram from 10 Downing Street to Richard Dales at the FCO, 9 June 1976.
28 Ibid.
29 BBC WAC PB306/324/1: Review of the Persian Service. Copy of Telegram No. 425 from the British Ambassador in Tehran to the FCO, *The Financial Times* and the BBC Persian Service, 30 June 1976.
30 BBC WAC E40/710/1: Review of the Persian Service, 9 November 1977.
31 Ibid.
32 Ibid.
33 Ibid.
34 Ibid.
35 Parviz Radji, *In the Service of the Peacock Throne* (London, 1983).
36 BBC WAC E58/25/1: 'BBC's "surprises" touch a new low in journalism', *Keyhan International*, 15 December 1977. Articles sent by Andrew Whitley from Tehran.
37 BBC WAC E40/656/1: Mark Dodd, BBC Eastern Service to Andrew Whitley, 5 January 1978.
38 Ibid.
39 FCO 8/3212: From Anthony Parsons to FCO, 25 January 1978, PRO.
40 Ibid.
41 Lutfali Khonji, interview with Massoumeh Torfeh, London University (SOAS), April 2008.
42 FCO 8/3212: Enclosed in report from Anthony Parsons to Middle East Department, FCO, 11 January 1978.
43 BBC WAC E40/840/1: Letter from Gerard Mansell to W. Deedes, editor of the *Daily Telegraph*, 3 January 1978.
44 BBC WAC E40/840/1: Letter from Gerard Mansell to Peter Temple Morris, MP, 4 December 1978.
45 BBC WAC E40/840/1: Persian complaints, 21 December 1978.
46 Ibid.
47 Lutfali Khonji, interview with Massoumeh Torfeh, London, 2008.
48 Ibid.
49 BBC Radio 4, *Document*, 24 March 2009.

50 FCO 8/3212: Report from British Embassy in Tehran to Middle East Department, FCO, 11 January 1978.

51 FCO 8/3212: Telegram from Anthony Parsons in Tehran, 15 December 1977.

52 Ibid.

53 BBC WAC E58/25/1: From Andrew Whitley to Head of Eastern Service, BBC World Service, 4 June 1976.

54 FCO 8/3213: Letter from J.H.G. Leahy at FCO to Gerard Mansell at the BBC, 19 April 1978.

55 FCO 8/3213: Exchanges between the FCO and BBC on Iran and the BBC, March to April 1978.

56 William H. Sullivan, *Mission to Iran* (New York, 1980), p. 156.

57 Ibid., pp. 156–7.

58 Ibid., p. 156.

59 Hedayatullah Matin Daftari, interview with Massoumeh Torfeh, Paris, 29 July 2010.

60 FCO 8/3214: Anthony Parsons to FCO, 25 September 1978.

61 John Simpson, *Behind Iranian Lines* (London, 1988), p. 18.

62 Ibid., pp. 13–14.

63 For a fuller description of how cassettes of Khomeini affected the power of his communication with the people of Iran and the success of the Iranian Revolution of 1979, see Annabelle Sreberny and Ali Mohammadi, *Small Media, Big Revolution: Communication, Culture, and the Iranian Revolution* (Minneapolis, MN, 1994).

64 Ahmad Salamatian, interview with Massoumeh Torfeh, Paris, 26 July 2010.

65 FCO8/3186: Anthony Parsons' confidential note to priority, FCO, Telegram No. 669, 11 October 1978.

66 Ibid.

67 Ibid.

68 FCO8/3184: British Embassy in Tehran to R.S. Gorham, MED, FCO, 1 August 1978.

69 At the Guadeloupe summit in 4–7 January 1979, the French President was in fact holding the key to an exceptionally important piece of information: the fact that the Shah was dying. Yet it remains unclear why he did not share it. The French President claims he was supportive of the Shah throughout when his British, American and German counterparts were all very pessimistic

about Iran. For example, he recalls the British Prime Minister Jim Callaghan saying at the summit that 'the Shah has lost, he no longer controls the situation' and US President Carter believing strongly that the army might take over once the Shah left. Giscard d'Estaing says he was surprised to hear the US putting so much hope in the army. Going against his European and American counterparts, the French President said that 'the Shah has asked us to offset the Soviet threat' and that 'even if weakened and isolated, we must support the Shah because he has a far more realistic view of what is to be done than any alternative figure'. He insists that it was Jimmy Carter who said that 'the situation has evolved and the Shah cannot stay' (Valéry Giscard d'Estaing, *Le Pouvoir et La Vie* (Paris, 1988), p. 110). Yet only two weeks before the Guadeloupe summit, Jimmy Carter had made an indirect attack on France for harbouring Khomeini. On 12 December, one day after the mass demonstrations on the Shi'i holy days of Tasua and Ashura, when President Carter still believed that the Shah could survive the storm, he expressed his anger at a press conference. 'The difficult situation there,' he said, referring to Iran, 'has been exacerbated by uncontrolled statements made from foreign nations that encourage bloodbath and violence. This is something that really is deplorable and, I would hope, would ease after this holy season passes' (Yonah Alexander and Allan Nanes, *The United States and Iran, A Documentary History* (Maryland, 1980), p. 464).

70   FCO8/3214: Anthony Parsons, confidential report No. 212/78 for the FCO, 9 October 1978.

71   FCO8/3214: 13 November 1978.

72   Ibid.

73   FCO8/3214: Anthony Parsons to FCO, 23 November 1978.

74   FCO8/3215: Anthony Parsons, Telegram No. 869, 27 November 1978.

75   FCO8/3215: Anthony Parsons, Telegram No. 868, 27 November 1978.

76   FCO8/3215: Anthony Parsons, Telegram No. 880 to FCO and Cabinet Office, 28 November 1978.

77   FCO8/3215: Anthony Parsons, Telegram No. 981 to FCO and Cabinet Office, 2 December 1978.

78   FCO8/3215: Anthony Parsons, Telegram No. 911 to FCO, 3 December 1978.

79   FCO8/3215: Anthony Parsons, Telegram No. 931 to FCO, 6 December 1978.

80   BBC WAC E40/840/1: Persian complaints. Letter from the Iranian Ambassador in London, Parviz C. Radji, to BBC Chairman, Sir Michael Swann, 21 December 1978.

81   Ibid.

82   Ibid.

83   FCO8/3212: Anthony Parsons to Middle East Department, FCO, 11 January 1978.

84   Ibid.

85   FCO8/3215: Iran's Image in the Media BBC, January to December 1978. Letter from C.J.S. Rundle, Research Department, FCO, to G.A. Pirie, British Embassy in Tehran, 20 December 1978.

86   Ibid.

87   BBC WAC E58/27/1: Persian Complaints, Part 3. Transcript of *World At One*, 26 October 1979.

88   Ibid.

89   Ibid.

90   BBC WAC E40/840/1: Letter from G.E.H. Mansell to John Junor, the editor of the *Sunday Express*, 17 November 1978.

91   BBC WAC E58/27/1: Persian Complaints, *Broadcast*, 11 June 1979.

92   Ibid.

93   BBC WAC E40/840/1: Letter from G.E.H. Mansell to John Junor, editor of the *Sunday Express*, 17 November 1978.

94   BBC Radio 4, *Document,* 24 March 2009.

95   Lutfali Khonji, interview with Massoumeh Torfeh, London, 2008.

96   BBC Witness Seminar: 'BBC Persian Service and the Iranian Revolution of 1979', 6 March 2010. See www.soas.ac.uk/centresof-fice/events/witness-seminar-iran (accessed 27 June 2013).

97   BBC WAC E40/840/1: Persian Complaints. Letter from Foreign Secretary David Owen, to BBC Chairman of BBC Board of Governors, Sir Michael Swann, 14 December 1978.

98   Ibid.

99   Ibid.

100 FCO8/3214: John H.G. Leahy of the FCO to BBC on Persian Service, 1 November 1978.

101 FCO8/3214: From David Owen to Tehran, Telegram No. 565, 9 November 1978.

102 Ibid.

103 BBC Persian Service Archives, programme for the 65th anniversary of the BBC Persian Service, produced by Shahryar Radpoor, an internally authorized account of the period.

104 BBC Radio 4, *Document,* 24 March 2009.

105 Ibid.

106 BBC Radio 4, *Document,* 24 March 2009.

107 FCO8/3215: Iran's Image in the Media BBC, January to December 1978. Letter from C.J.S. Rundle, Research Department, FCO, to G.A. Pirie, British Embassy in Tehran, 20 December 1978.

108 Ibid.

109 Ibid.

110 Ibid. See also Al Jazeera, 'Iran's media: The new red lines', Listening Post episode, 2 February 2013. Available at www.aljazeera.com/programmes/listeningpost/2013/02/201321195034218716.html (accessed 11 September 2013).

111 Ervand Abrahamian, *Iran Between Two Revolutions* (Princeton, NJ, 1982), p. 522.

112 FCO 8/3215: Iran's Image in the Media, BBC, January to December 1978, 14 December 1978.

113 BBC WAC E40/840/1: Letter from BBC Managing Director of External Broadcasting, Gerard Mansell to W. Deedes, Editor, *Daily Telegraph*, 3 January 1979.

114 Lutfali Khonji, interview with Massoumeh Torfeh, London, 2008.

115 Sreberny and Mohammadi, *Small Media, Big Revolution*, chapter 9.

116 Other interviews with BBC Persian Service staff, including Shahran Tabari and Solmaz Dabiri.

117 Mehrdad Khonsari, interview with Massoumeh Torfeh for the BBC Witness Seminar, Centre for Media and Film Studies, SOAS, 6 March 2010.

118 Radji, *In the Service of the Peacock Throne*, p. 271.

119 BBC Radio 4, *Document*, 2009.

120 BBC Radio 4, *Document*, 2009.

121 Radji, *In the Service of the Peacock Throne*, p. 167.

122 Ibid.

123 FCO8/3215: Iran's Image in the Media, BBC, 13 December 1978.

124 Ibid.

125 FCO8/3186: The Recent Disturbances in Iran. Sir Anthony Parsons to the Secretary of State for Foreign and Commonwealth Affairs. Diplomatic Report No. 212/78, 9 October 1978.

126 Mohammad Reza Pahlavi, *The Shah's Story* (London, 1980) (translated by Teresa Waugh), p. 163.

127 Ibid.

128 FCO8/3185: I.T.M. Lucas, Middle Eastern Department, speaking notes for Cabinet meeting on 14 September, 13 September 1978.

129 Ibid.

130 Ibid.

131 Ibid.

132 FCO8/3186: David Owen to British Embassy in Tehran, Telegram No. 654, 12 October 1978.

133 FCO8/3185: Letter from Prime Minister James Callaghan in Downing Street to His Imperial Majesty Mohammad Reza Pahlavi *Shahanshah Aryamehr*, 14 September 1978.

134 FCO8/3184: Jay [the only name on document] for FCO and Whitehall, 8 September 1978.

135 FCO8/3216: Confidential report by B.L. Crowe, Planning Staff for Mr Gorham, MED, FCO, Anglo–American Planning Talks on Iran, held on 10 October 1978 in Washington, DC, 12 October 1978.

136 Ibid.

137 FCO8/3188: From R.J.S. Muir in FCO to Mr Carrick, 7 December 1978.

138 Sullivan, *Mission to Iran*, p. 212.

139 Ibid.

140 Ibid., p. 225.

141 Ibid., p. 226.

142 Full accounts of the Shah's well-kept secret about his cancer are offered in David Owen's book, *In Sickness and in Power* (London, 2009); and in Farah Pahlavi's *An Enduring Love* (New York, 2004).

143 Giscard d'Estaing, *Le Pouvoir et la Vie*, pp. 108–10.

144 Sullivan, *Mission to Iran*, p. 230.

145 Sullivan, *Mission to Iran*, p. 287.

146 FCO8/3189: Note for Cabinet: 14 December: Iran: Line to Take, 14 December 1978.

147 BBC WAC E58/26/1: Persian Complaints Part 2, 2 March 1979.

Chapter 5: BBC Broadcasting to Afghanistan

 1 See *Encyclopaedia Britannica*, 'Pashtun' article. Available at www.
   britannica.com/EBchecked/topic/445546/Pashtun (accessed 1
   July 2013).
 2 Gordon Adam, 'Radio in Afghanistan: Socially useful communications in wartime', in O. Hemer and T. Tufte (eds), *Media and
   Global Change* (Buenos Aires, 2005).
 3 *BBC Annual Review 2002–2003* (London, 2003).
 4 *The Times* archives, 30 July 1941, report from Our Own
   Correspondent [Possibly Ann Lambton].
 5 BBC WAC E58/30/1: FCO to Oliver Whitley, director of External
   Broadcasting, 18 February 1969.
 6 BBC WAC E58/25/1: 7 April 1971.
 7 BBC WAC E40/656/1: Persian Complaints.
 8 BBC WAC E58/30/1: Pashto 1971–9, 14 December 1971.
 9 Ibid.
10 Report by Andrew Whitley of the BBC in Teheran, 30 January
   1974.
11 Ibid.
12 FCO82762: Information Policy Report, July 1974.
13 FCO2762.
14 FCO2762.
15 BBC WAC E58/30/1: Pashto 1971–9, 27 August 1974.
16 David Page, interview with Massoumeh Torfeh at London
   University (SOAS), 16 September 2008.
17 Ibid.
18 Ibid.
19 Gordon Adam, interview with Massoumeh Torfeh, The Front Line
   Club, 5 August 2008.
20 Ibid.
21 Ibid.
22 Ibid.
23 Languages Other Than English.
24 William Crawley, interview with Massoumeh Torfeh at London
   University (SOAS), 21 July 2008.

25   Ahmad Rashid, *Descent into Chaos* (London, 2009), p. 11.

26   Ahmad Rashid, *Taliban* (London, 2001), p. 2.

27   Baqer Moin, interview with Massoumeh Torfeh in Sloan Square, London, 21 January 2009.

28   A conference held by the Centre for Media and Film Studies at SOAS, 'Communicating with the Persian Speaking World', held on 6 June 2008, dealt with the subject in detail. For more information, see www.soas.ac.uk/mediaandfilm/events/06jun2008-communicating-with-the-persian-speaking-world---day-1.html (accessed 1 July 2013).

29   InterMedia survey of 3,903 adult male heads of household conducted between 29 November 1997 and 27 February 1998.

30   Emma Brockes, 'A long way from Ambridge', *Guardian*, 23 October 2001.

31   The UK Parliament, Minutes of Evidence for the Select Committee on Foreign Affairs, Supplementary Memorandum for BBC World Service, February 2001.

32   Reporters Without Borders, 14 March 2001.

33   Ibid.

34   *BBC Annual Reports and Accounts for 1997–98 for the Board of Governors* (London, 1998).

35   Rashid, *Descent into Chaos*, p. 17.

36   BBC website (South Asia section), 'Afghans hooked on BBC', 20 September 2001. Available at http://news.bbc.co.uk/1/hi/world/south_asia/1555030.stm (accessed 1 July 2013).

37   Behrouz Afagh, interview with Massoumeh Torfeh, BBC Bush House, 22 December 2008.

38   Afagh, interview, 22 December 2008.

39   Moin, interview, 21 January 2009.

40   Massoumeh Torfeh recalls these daily interviews when she was working in the BBC Persian and Pashto Service at the time.

41   BBC press release, 'BBC World Service wins top Commonwealth Broadcasting Association honour and commendation from Tony Blair', 2 May 2002. Available at www.bbc.co.uk/pressoffice/press-releases/stories/2002/05_may/02/worldservice_award.shtml (accessed 1 July 2013).

42   K. Parkinson, *Afghanistan at a Glance* (London, 2008) (BBC Marketing, Communications and Audiences), p. 2.

43   Ibid.

44   Afagh, interview, 22 December 2008.
45   Parkinson, *Afghanistan at a Glance*, p. 1.
46   BBC Media Action, 'Afghanistan's Open Jirga'. Available at www. bbc.co.uk/mediaaction/where_we_work/asia/afghanistan/ afghanistan_open_jirga.html (accessed 10 September 2013).

Chapter 6: Culture Wars as Foreign Policy: BBC Persian Television and the Islamic Republic of Iran

1   Nigel Chapman, director of BBC World Service, cited in BBC news article, 'BBC to launch TV channel for Iran', 10 October 2006. Available at http://news.bbc.co.uk/1/hi/entertainment/6037832. stm (accessed 3 July 2013).
2   BBC Media Centre, 'BBC Persian audiences nearly double in Iran despite continued censorship', 2 April 2013. Available at www.bbc. co.uk/mediacentre/latestnews/2013/persian-arabic-audiences- rise.html (accessed 10 September 2013).
3   Behrouz Afagh, personal communication with Annabelle Sreberny, 3 April 2013.
4   Behrouz Afagh, interview with Massoumeh Torfeh, BBC Bush House, 22 December 2008.
5   BBC website: press release 'The BBC in the Arab world'. Available at http://www.bbc.co.uk/pressoffice/pressreleases/stories/2008/03_ march/03/arabic_worldservice.shtml (accessed 3 July 2013).
6   Ibid.
7   Richard Sambrook, BBC website: news: the editors, 14 January 2009. Available at www.bbc.co.uk/blogs/theeditors/2009/01/bbc_ persian_tv.html (accessed 3 July 2013).
8   Stephen Williams, 'The power of TV news: An insider's perspec- tive on the launch of BBC Persian TV in the year of the Iranian uprising', Discussion Paper Series No. D-54, Joan Shorenstein Center on the Press, Politics and Public Policy, Harvard University (2010).
9   Reporters without Borders, 2011.
10   Rooz Online, 'The Culture Ministry issued warning again', 28 October 2008. Available at www.roozonline.com/persian/archive/ archivenews/news/archive/2008/october/28/article/-8174ad88cd. html (accessed 3 July 2013).

11   Ali Asghar Ramezanpoor, interview with Massoumeh Torfeh, London, November 2011.

12   IRIB website: About Us, 'IRIB at a glance'. Available at www.irib.ir/English/AboutUs/index.php (accessed 3 July 2013).

13   Ibid.

14   Ibid.

15   Sahar website: About Us. Available at http://english.sahartv.ir/aboutus-73 (accessed 3 July 2013).

16   Ibid.

17   Press TV website: About Us. Available at www.presstv.ir/about.html (accessed 3 July 2013).

18   Bahari has written about his experiences in *Then They Came for Me: A Family's Story of Love, Captivity and Survival* (London, 2011); and made a documentary, 'Forced Confessions', 2013.

19   Rooz Online, 'BBC Persian TV is not appropriate for the country's security'. 15 January 2009. Available at www.roozonline.com/persian/archive/overall-archive/news/archive/2009/january/15/article/-385aa8df52.html (accessed 3 July 2013).

20   Parsian Forum, 'Zarghami's reaction to the launch of BBC', 19 January 2009. Available at www.parsianforum.com/archive/index.php/t-17967.html (accessed 3 July 2013).

21   Borjian, Maryam, 'The rise and fall of a partnership: The British Council and the Islamic Republic of Iran (2001–09)', *Iranian Studies* 44/4 (2011), pp. 541–62.

22   For further description, see Annabelle Sreberny and Gholam Khiabany, *Blogistan* (London, 2010).

23   Mehr News, 'The enemies are plotting against Iran through the soft war', 9 July 2009. Available at Mehr News Agency website: www.mehrnews.com/fa/newsdetail.aspx?NewsID=909025 (accessed 6 November 2011).

24   Mardomak, 'Ayatollah Khamenei's concern over social science courses in universities', 31 August 2009. Available at www.mardomak.org/story/44060 (accessed 6 November 2011).

25   Mardomak, 'Armed Forces set up a soft war task force', 5 October 2009. Available at www.mardomak.org/story/45377 (accessed 6 November 2011).

26   Fars News web page: 'Today our priority is to confront soft war', Ali Khamenie, 25 November 2009.

27 Mardomak, 'Confronting the soft war is the country's first priority', 25 November 2009. Available at www.mardomak.org/story/47018 (accessed 6 November 2013).

28 Iranian UK, 'Zarghami's strange claim: Neda's death picture is a phony', 4 July 2009. Available at www.iranuk88.com/article. php?id=39219 (accessed 3 July 2013).

29 Jaras, Mohammad Javad Larijani, 'The British Intelligence Service has killed Neda Agha Sultan', 19 November 2010. Available at Rah-e-Sabz Jaras: www.rahesabz.net/story/27595 (accessed 29 October 2011).

30 Tabnak, pro-government newspaper, 'BBC Correspondent killed Neda', 25 June 2009. Available at www.tabnak.ir/fa/pages/?cid=52956 (accessed 29 October 2011).

31 Kaleme, 'Neda Agha Sultan's mother's reaction to Ahmadinejad's comments: People in Iran and the world know who killed Neda', 25 September 2011. Available at www.kaleme.com/1390/07/03/klm-74448/?theme=fast (accessed 29 October 2011).

32 Williams, 'The power of TV news', p. 6.

33 AFP, 'BBC says its satellite broadcasts being disrupted from Iran', 14 June 2009. Available at Radio Netherlands Worldwide: http://blogs.rnw.nl/medianetwork/bbc-says-its-satellite-broad-casts-being-disrupted-from-iran (accessed 3 July 2013).

34 AFP, 'BBC says Persian service being jammed', 20 December 2009. Available from Google News: www.google.com/hostednews/afp/article/ALeqM5iA4FLs8IFv5khU_lOB8-Njt2CgIg (accessede 3 July 2013).

35 BBC World Service Press Office, 'BBC adds more satellites for its Persian TV service', 19 June 2009. Available from Radio Netherlands Worldwide: http://blogs.rnw.nl/medianetwork/bbc-adds-more-satellites-for-its-persian-tv-service (accessed 3 July 2013).

36 BBC Press Office, 'BBC Persian television broadcasting despite interference from Iran', 21 December 2009. Available at http://www.bbc.co.uk/pressoffice/pressreleases/stories/2009/12_december/21/persian.shtml (accessed 3 July 2013).

37 BBC Media Centre, 'Satellite and internet jamming rises as broadcast industry seek to uphold UN Article 19', 20 November 2012. Available at www.bbc.co.uk/mediacentre/latestnews/2012/201112 wsjammingconference.html (accessed 3 July 2013).

37 Small Media, 'Satellite jamming in Iran: A war over airwaves', November 2012. Available at http://smallmedia.org.uk/sites/default/files/Satellite%20Jamming.pdf (accessed 3 July 2013).

39 Radio Zamaneh, Publication of a list of 60 organizations connected to the 'soft war', 4 January 2010. Available at http://zamaaneh.com/news/2010/01/_60_2.html (accessed 28 October 2011).

40 BBC website, Ayatollah Khamenei documentary, 17 September 2011 (in Persian). Available at www.bbc.co.uk/persian/iran/2011/09/110916_l72_lf_ayatollah_ways_online.shtml (accessed 3 July 2013).

41 For the full visual impact of what such jamming looks like, see www.youtube.com/watch?v=Kgw2bv9eCdY&feature=player_embedded (accessed 3 July 2013).

42 M. Shojaie, 'Six documentary makers, victims of Islamic Republic's retaliation from BBC?', 19 September 2011 (in Persian). Available from Deutsche Welle: www.dw-world.de/dw/article/0,,15399440,00.html (accessed 3 July 2013).

43 Ibid.

44 After Rouhani's election victory July 2013, all film-makers still detained were released.

45 See the list at www.facebook.com/notes/peace-solh/the-list-of-withdrawn-movies-from-cinema-verite-festival-in-iran/270504566326741 (accessed 3 July 2013).

46 His comments and many others can be found at www.facebook.com/notes/peace-solh/the-list-of-withdrawn-movies-from-cinema-verite-festival-in-iran/270504566326741 (accessed 3 July 2013).

47 His comments and many others are available at http://www.facebook.com/notes/peace-solh/the-list-of-withdrawn-movies-from-cinema-verite-festival-in-iran/270504566326741 (accessed 11 July 2013).

48 Hamshahri Online, 'Members of BBC-affiliated network arrested', 20 September 2011 (in Persian). Available at http://hamshahrion-line.ir/news-146183.aspx (accessed 3 July 2013).

49 Ramezanpoor, interview with Massoumeh Torfeh, November 2011.

50 Cited on Fars News website: Mr. Majid Ansari, 'Remember Imam was opposed to Voice of America', 20 November 2010.

51   Hamshahri Online, 'The Intelligence Minister warned BBC-affiliated elements', 25 September 2011. Available at http://hamshahrionline.ir/news-146566.aspx (accessed 3 July 2013).

52   Radio Farda, 'BBC and VOA are extensions of American intelligence services', 21 October 2011. Available at www.radiofarda.com/content/f10_iran_police_chief_says_bbc_and_voa_are_connceted_to_usa_intelligence/24367075.html (accessed 3 July 2013).

53   Young Journalists Club, 'BBC was extensively using its element in Iran', 18 September 2011 (in Persian). Available at www.yjc.ir/portal/NewsDesc.aspx?newsid=514640 (accessed 3 July 2013).

54   Head of House of Cinema's letter to Iranian Documentary Film Association, 4 October 2011. Available from Iranian Documentary Film Association: http://irandocfilm.org/2akhbar.asp?ID=1845 (accessed 3 July 2013).

55   Deutsche Welle, 'The head of Cinema House's press conference on arrested documentary makers', 26 September 2011 (in Persian). Available at http://www.dw-world.de/dw/article/0,,15417688,00.html (accessed 3 July 2013).

56   Broadcasting Board of Governors, 'BBC-BBG joint protest of threats to the independent media in Iran', 23 September 2011. Available at www.bbg.gov/blog/2011/09/23/bbc-bbg-joint-protest-of-threats-to-the-independent-media-in-iran (accessed 3 July 2013).

57   Peter Horrocks, BBC website: news: the editors: 'Families of BBC staff being harassed in Iran', 5 October 2011. Available at www.bbc.co.uk/blogs/theeditors/2011/10/families_of_bbc_staff.html (accessed 3 July 2013).

58   Ramezanpoor, interview with Massoumeh Torfeh, November 2011.

59   Thomas Erdbrink, 'In Iran, what's forbidden is in – and on Rupert Murdoch's Farsi1 TV channel', Washington Post Foreign Service, 26 June 2010. Available at www.washingtonpost.com/wp-dyn/content/article/2010/06/25/AR2010062504356.html (accessed 3 July 2013).

60   Dexter Filkins, 'TV channel draws viewers, and threats, in Iran', *New York Times*, 19 November 2010. Available at www.nytimes.com/2010/11/20/world/middleeast/20afghan.html (accessed 3 July 2013).

61   Marjan TV Network website: www.marjantvnetwork.com (accessed 3 July 2013).

62   This is by no means a complete listing of television channels available in Iran. For this, look at www.glwiz.com, which lists 42 channels; or www.iran.tv/site/index.php and www.gooyauk.com/tv.html, which provides links to many online channels.

63   See Annabelle Sreberny and Massoumeh Torfeh (eds), *Cultural Revolution in Iran: Contemporary Popular Culture in the Islamic Republic* (London, 2013).

64   Liliane Landor, 'Statement regarding BBC Persian', 13 June 2013. Available at http://www.bbc.co.uk/mediacentre/statements/bbc-persian-statement.html (accessed 11 July 2013).

65   This section draws on Annabelle Sreberny's participant observation of the BBC PTV team for a month before the election.

66   Medhi Parpanchi, interview at Broadcasting House, 2 June 2013.

67   Informal discussion with BBC PTV staff, Broadcasting House, 28 May 2013.

68   Thanks to Jenny Norton, Planning Editor, Near East Hub, BBC World Service, for the accuracy of this detail. Personal communication, 10 July 2013.

69   Thomas Erdbrink, 'President-elect of Iran says he will engage with the West', 29 June 2013. Available at http://www.nytimes.com/2013/06/30/world/middleeast/president-elect-of-iran-says-he-will-engage-with-the-west.html?_r=0 (accessed 11 July 2013).

70   BBC News, 'Rouhani urges end to meddling in Iranians' private lives', 3 July 2013. Available at http://www.bbc.co.uk/news/world-middle-east-23161972 (accessed 11 July 2013).

Conclusion

1   BBC, Broadcasting House mini-site. Available at http://www.bbc.co.uk/broadcastinghouse (accessed 11 July 2013).

2   Over the summer of 2013, there has been a 'Public Consultation on BBC Trust governance of BBC World Service, via an operating licence'. Available at www.bbc.co.uk/bbctrust/have_your_say/world_service.html (accessed 9 October 2013). It remains to be seen what recommendations emerge.

Bibliography

Abrahamian, Ervand, *Iran Between Two Revolutions* (Princeton, NJ, 1982).

Adam, Gordon, 'Radio in Afghanistan: Socially useful communications in wartime', in O. Hemer and T. Tufte (eds), *Media and Global Change* (Buenos Aires, 2005).

Adelkhah, Nima, 'Iran integrates the concept of "soft war" into its strategic planning', *Jamestown Foundation Terrorism Monitor* 8/23 (2010). Available at www.jamestown.org/programs/tm/ archivesgta/2010 (accessed 5 July 2013).

Afrasiabi, Bahram, *Mossadeq and History* (Tehran, 1979).

Alam, Asadollah, *The Shah and I* (London, 2008).

Alexander, Yonah and Nanes, Allan, *The United States and Iran, A Documentary History* (Maryland, 1980).

Amr, Hady, *The Need to Communicate: How to Improve US Public Diplomacy with the Islamic World* (Washington, DC, 2004).

Anderson, Matilda, Gillespie, Marie and Mackay, Hugh, 'Mapping digital diasporas @ BBC World Service: users and uses of the Persian and Arabic websites', *Middle East Journal of Culture and Communication* 3/2 (2013), pp. 256–78.

Armitage, Richard L. and Nye, Joseph S., Jr, *CSIS Commission on Smart Power: A Smarter, More Secure America* (Washington, DC, 2007).

Borjian, Maryam, 'The rise and fall of a partnership: The British Council and the Islamic Republic of Iran (2001–09)', *Iranian Studies* 44/4 (2011), pp. 541–62.

Briggs, Asa, *The History of Broadcasting in the United Kingdom, Vol. 3: The War of Words* (Oxford, 1995).

Bullard, Reader S., *Britain and the Middle East*, Third Revised Edition (London, 1964).

Dutta-Bergman, Mohan, 'U.S. public diplomacy in the Middle East: A critical cultural approach', *Journal of Communication Inquiry* 30/2 (2006), pp. 102–24.

Elm, Mostafa, *Oil, Power and Principle: Iran's Oil Nationalization and its Aftermath* (Syracuse, 1992).

Elwell-Sutton, Laurence Paul, *Persian Oil: A Study in Power Politics* (London, 1955).

Giscard d'Estaing, Valéry, *Le Pouvoir et La Vie* (Paris, 1988).

El Issawi, Fatima and Baumann, Gerd, 'The BBC Arabic Service: changing political mediascapes', *Middle East Journal of Culture and Communication* 3/2 (2010), pp. 137–51.

Keddie, Nikki R., *Modern Iran, Roots and Results of Revolution* (New Haven, CT, 2006).

Kemp, Norman, *Abadan: A First-Hand Account of the Persian Oil Crisis* (London, 1953).

Kinzer, Stephen, *All the Shah's Men: An American Coup and the Roots of Middle East Terror* (Princeton, NJ, 2008).

Leonard, Mark and Small, Andrew with Rose, Martin, *British Public Diplomacy in the 'Age of Schisms'* (London, 2005).

Leonard, Mark, Stead, Catherine and Smewing, Conrad, *Public Diplomacy* (London, 2002).

Milani, Abbas, *The Shah* (New York, 2011).

Nye, Joseph, *Soft Power: The Means to Success in World Politics* (New York, 2004).

Pahlavi, Farah, *An Enduring Love: My Life with the Shah* (New York, 2004).

Pahlavi, Mohammed Reza, *The Shah's Story* (London, 1980).

Owen, David, *In Sickness and In Power: Illness in Heads of Government During the Last 100 Years* (London, 2009).

Pamment, James, *New Public Diplomacy in the 21st Century* (Abingdon and New York, 2012).

Parkinson, K., *Afghanistan at a Glance* (London, 2008) (BBC Marketing, Communications and Audiences).

Partner, Peter, *Arab Voices: The BBC Arabic Service 1938–1988* (London, 1988).

Radji, Parviz, *In the Service of the Peacock Throne* (London, 1983).

Rashid, Ahmad, *Descent into Chaos* (London, 2009).

Roosevelt, Kermit, *Counter Coup: The Struggle for the Control of Iran* (New York, 1979).

Schiller, Herb, 'Not yet the Post-Imperial Era', *Critical Studies in Mass Communication* 8/1 (1991).

Shahidi, Hossein, 'The BBC Persian Service, 1940–1953', *Journal of Iranian Research and Analysis* 17/1 (2001).

Simpson, John, *Behind Iranian Lines* (London, 1988).

Sreberny, Annabelle, 'Too soft on "soft war": Commentary on Monroe Price's "Iran and the Soft War"', *International Journal of Communication* 7 (2013), Feature 801–4. Available at http://eprints.soas.ac.uk/15696/1/AS%20IoJC%202004-8001-1-PB.pdf (accessed 11 September 2013).

Sreberny, Annabelle and Khiabany, Gholam, *Blogistan* (London, 2010).

Sreberny, Annabelle and Torfeh, Massoumeh, 'The BBC Persian Service 1979', *Historical Journal of Film, Radio and Television* 28/4 (2008), pp. 515–35.

Sreberny, Annabelle and Torfeh, Massoumeh, 'The BBC World Service from wartime propaganda to public diplomacy: the case of Iran', in M. Gillespie and A. Webb (eds), *Diasporas and Diplomacy: Cosmopolitan Contact Zones at the BBC World Service (1932–2012)* (New York and London, 2013).

Sreberny-Mohammadi, Annabelle and Mohammadi, Ali, *Small Media, Big Revolution: Communication, Culture, and the Iranian Revolution* (Minneapolis, MN, 1994).

Sullivan, William H., *Mission to Iran* (New York, 1981).

Torfeh, Massoumeh and Sreberny, Annabelle, 'Broadcasting to Afghanistan: A history of the BBC Pashto Service', in 'The BBC and Public Diplomacy in the Middle East', special issue of *Middle East Journal of Culture and Communication* 3/2 (2010), pp. 192–215.

Torfeh, Massoumeh and Sreberny, Annabelle, 'The BBC Persian Service and the Islamic Revolution of 1979', in 'The BBC and Public Diplomacy in the Middle East', special issue of *Middle East Journal of Culture and Communication* 3/2 (2010), pp. 216–41.

Tuch, Hans N., *Communicating with the World: U.S. Public Diplomacy Overseas* (New York, 1990).

Walker, Andrew, *A Skyful of Freedom: 60 Years of the BBC World Service* (London, 1992).

Wang, Jian and Chang, Tsan-Kuo, 'Strategic public diplomacy and local press: How a high profile "head-of-state" visit was covered in America's heartland', *Public Relations Review* 30 (2004), pp. 11–24.

Warnaar, Maaike, *So Many Similarities: Linking Domestic Dissent to Foreign Threat in Iran*. Working Paper No. 20, Knowledge Programme Civil Society in West Asia, HIVOS and Amsterdam Institute for Social Science Research (AISSR), University of Amsterdam (2011).

Williams, Stephen, 'The power of TV news: An insider's perspective on the launch of BBC Persian TV in the year of the Iranian uprising', Discussion Paper Series No. D-54, Joan Shorenstein Center on the Press, Politics and Public Policy, Harvard University (2010).

Wright, Denis, *The English Amongst the Persians* (London, 1977).

Wright, Denis, *The Persians Amongst the English* (London, 1985).

Interviews (all conducted by Massoumeh Torfeh)

Gordon Adam: former head of BBC Pashto Service.

Behrouz Afagh: head of BBC Asia Pacific Region.

Abolhassan Bani-Sadr: the first president of the Islamic Republic of Iran.

William Crawley: former head of the BBC Eastern Service.

Professor Fred Halliday: writer and professor of international relations.

Darioush Homayoun: minister of information 1978–9.

Dr Mehrdad Khonsary: former press attaché at the Embassy of Iran 1978.

Hedayat Matin-Daftari: Freedom Front politician and lawyer.

Baqer Moin: former head of the BBC Persian & Pashto Service.

Lord David Owen: former British foreign secretary.

David Page: former deputy head of the Eastern Service.

Ali Asghar Ramezanpoor: communications chief to President Mohammad Khatami.

Ahmad Salamatian: former member of the Parliament of the Islamic Republic of Iran.
Khosrow Shakery: historian of Iran's labour movement.

Radio archives

BBC Persian Service Archives, programme for the 65th anniversary of the BBC Persian Service, produced by Shahryar Radpoor.

Index